ILLUSTRATED BY:
LAURA LIVI

DESIGNED BY:
LAURA LIVI & CORRADO SESSELEGO

COLOR IT WITH FLOWERS! - POCKET BOOK. © 2019 BLUE MONKEY STUDIO
(PUBLISHED THROUGH THE ZENITH BOOKS PUBLISHING LINE)

ALL ARTWORK © 2016-2019 BLUE MONKEY STUDIO

COLOR IT WITH FLOWERS!

Pocket Book!

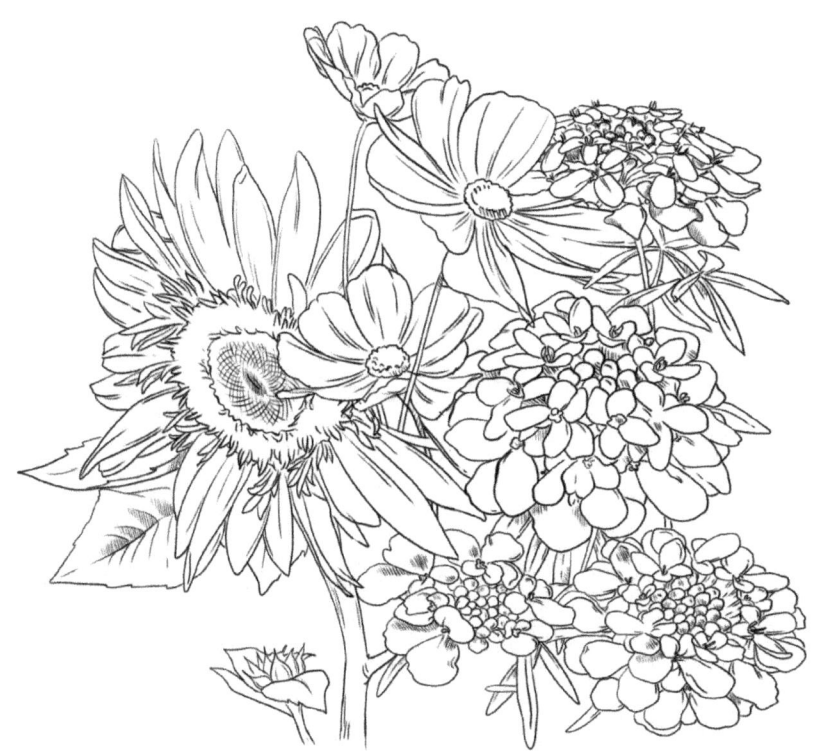

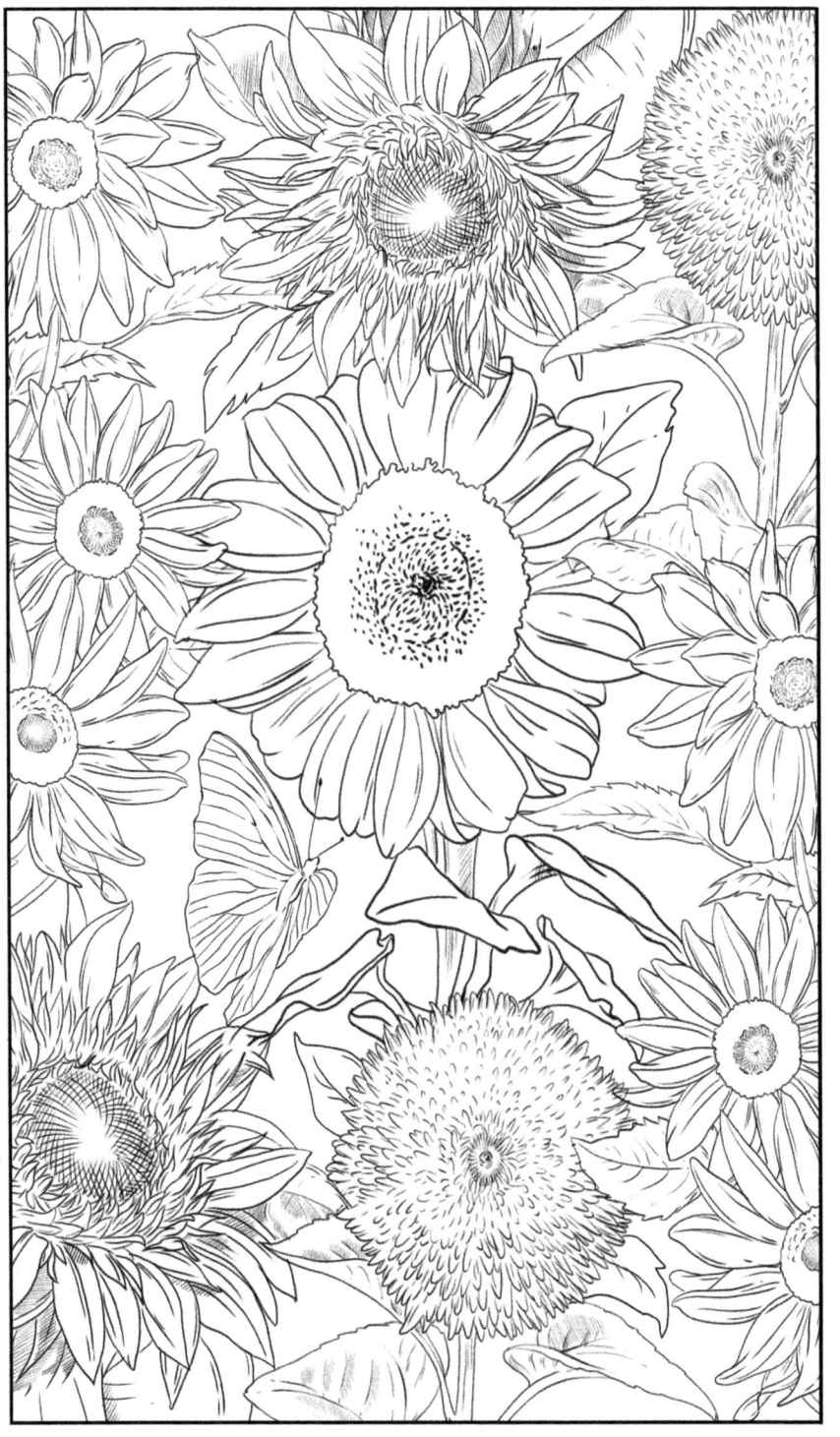

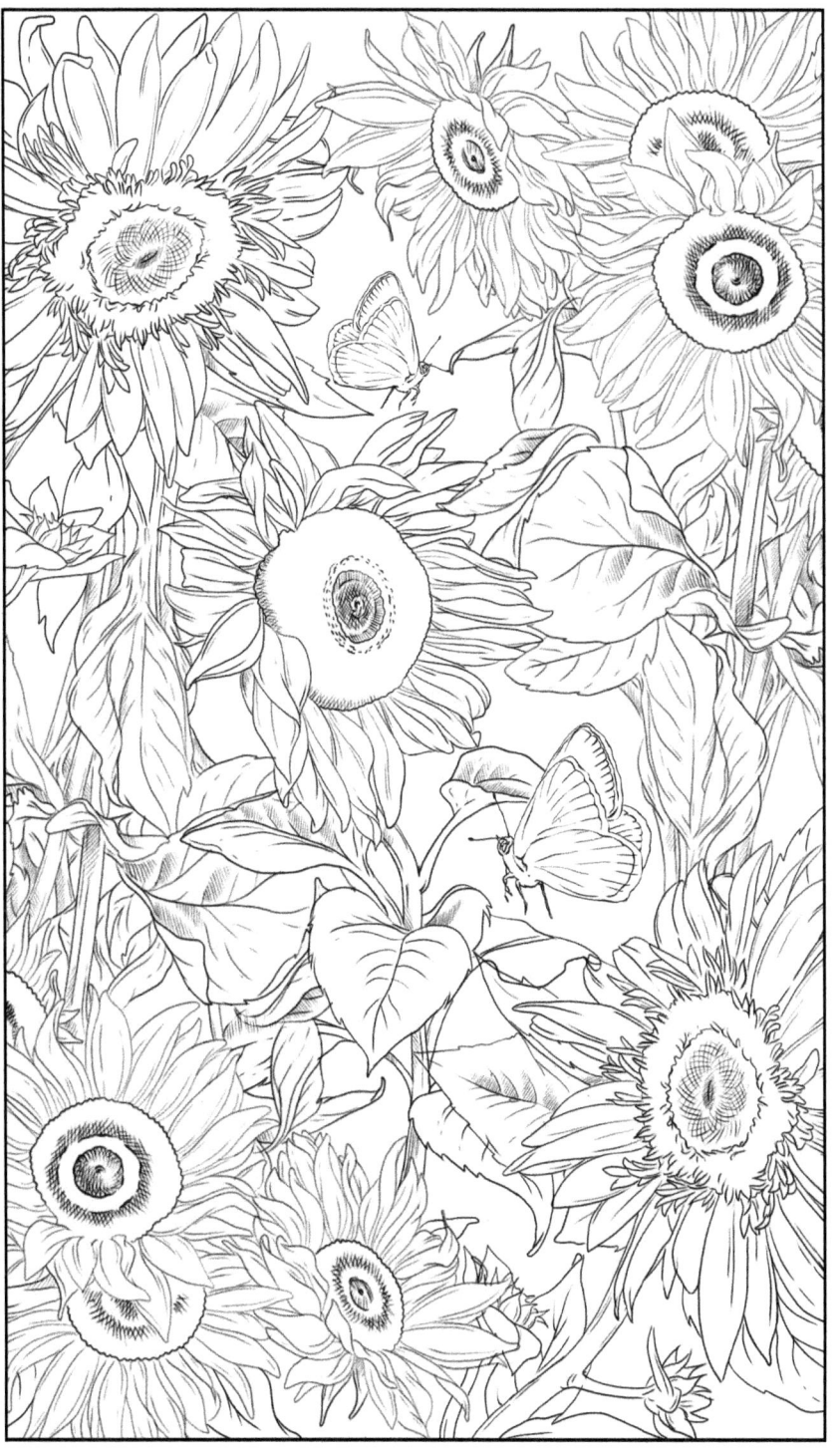

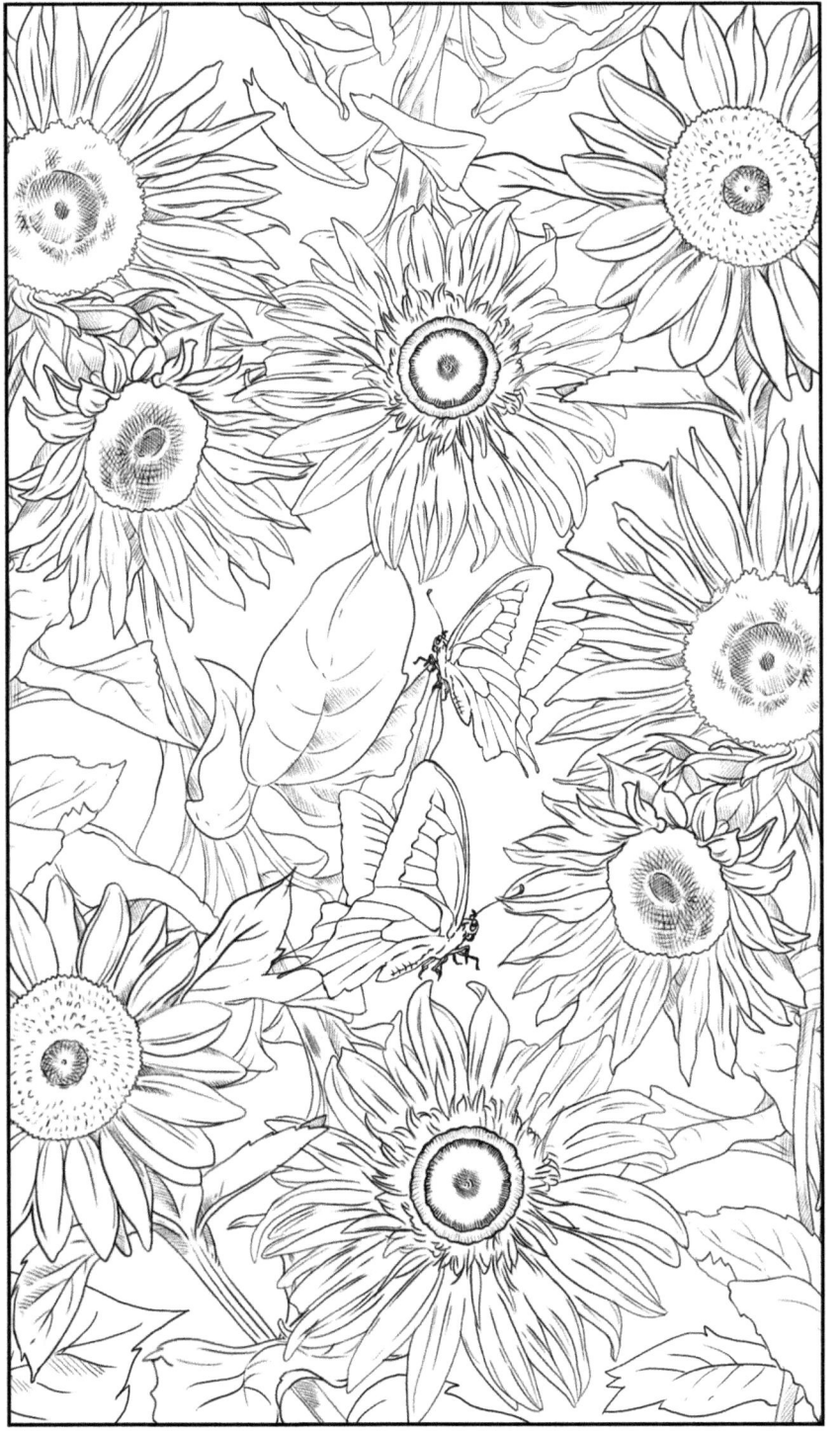

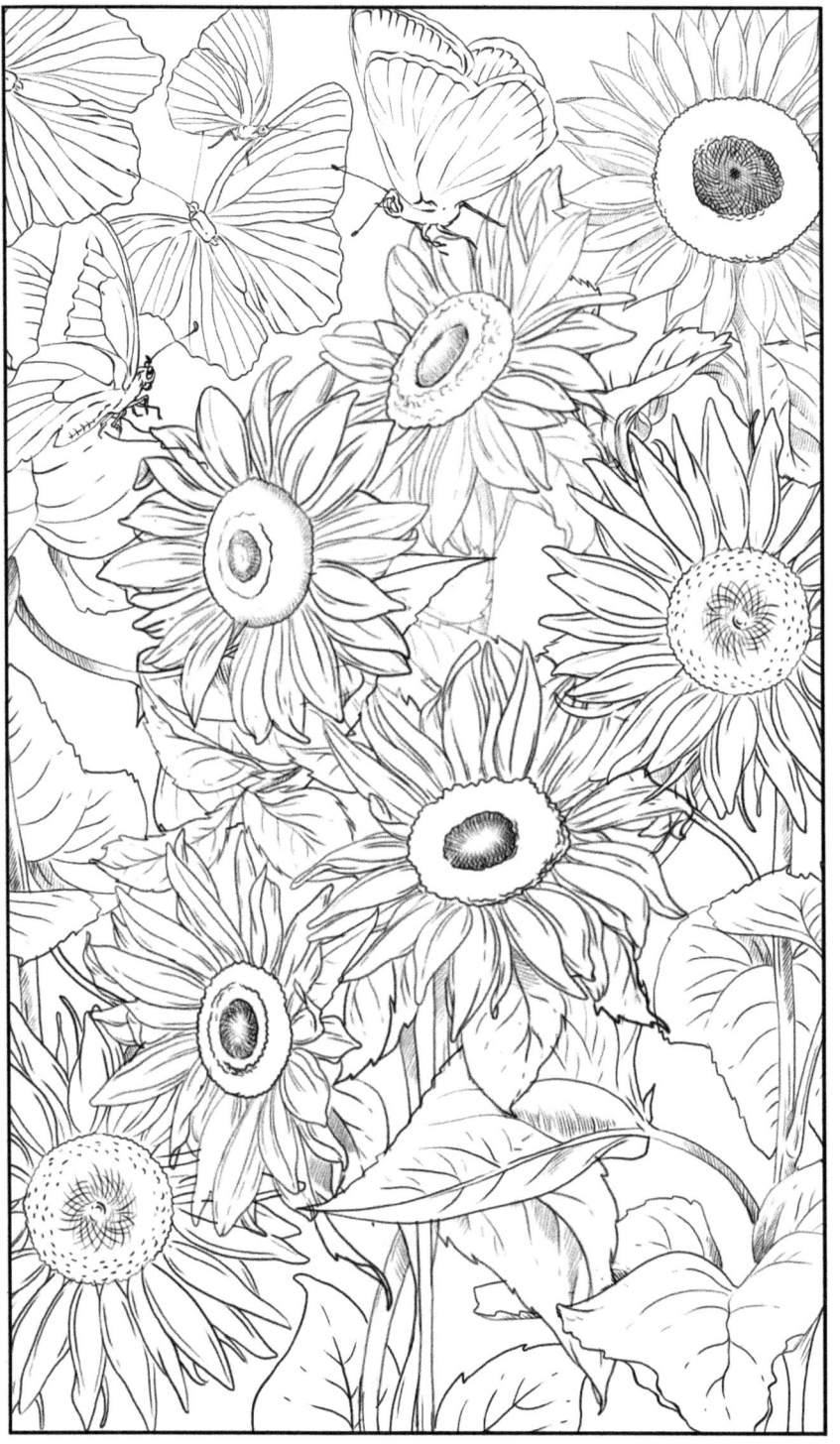

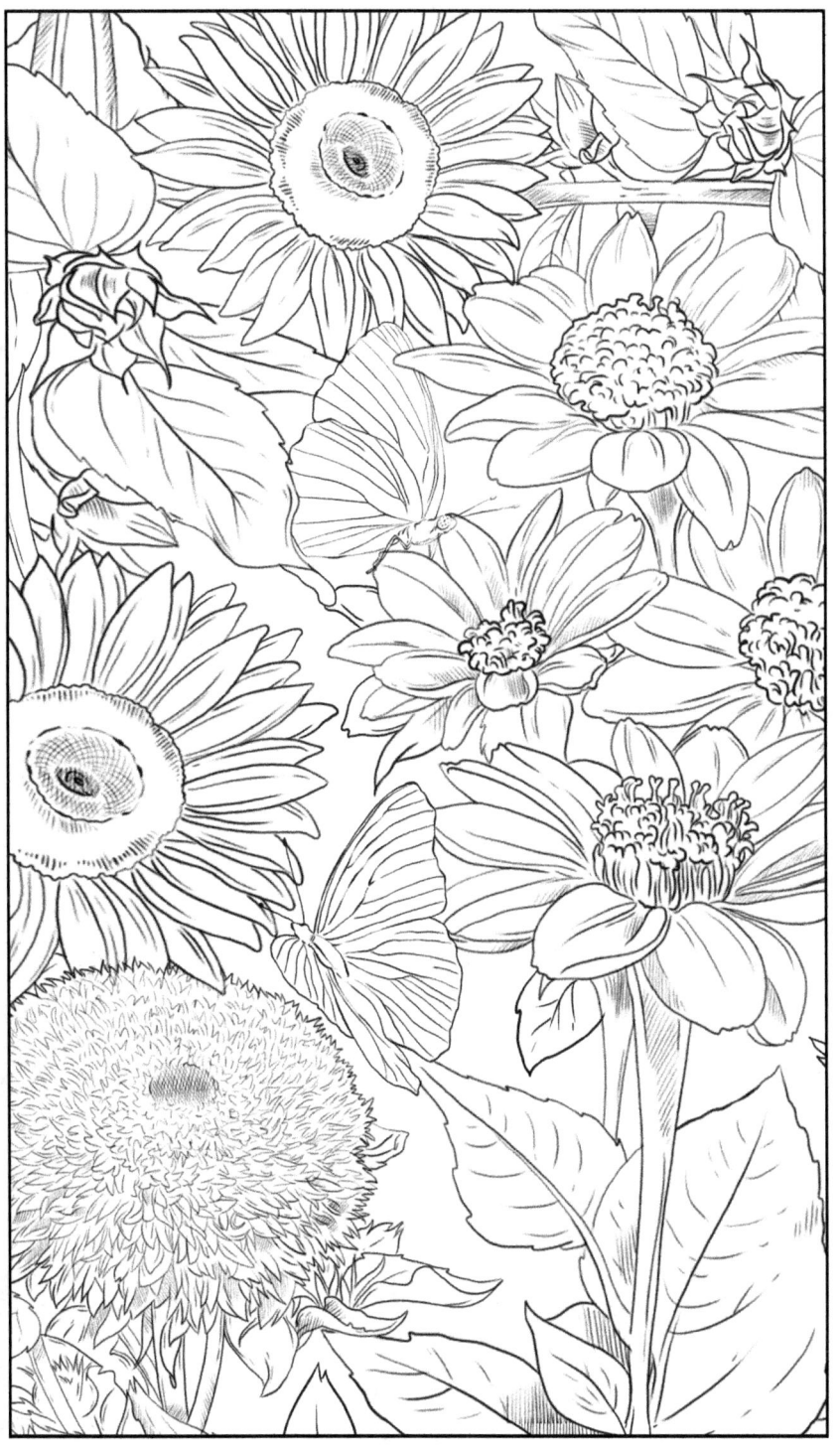

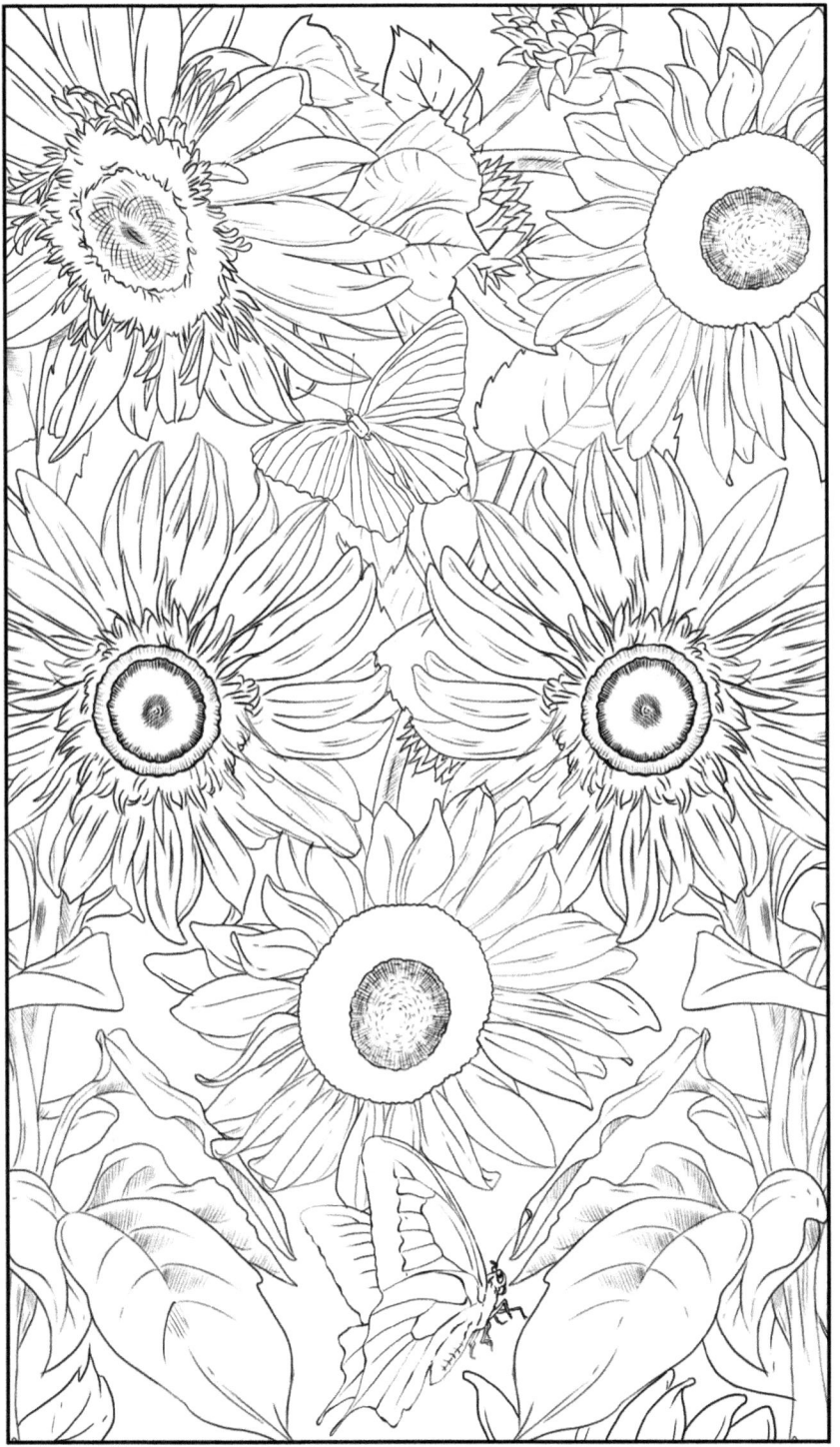

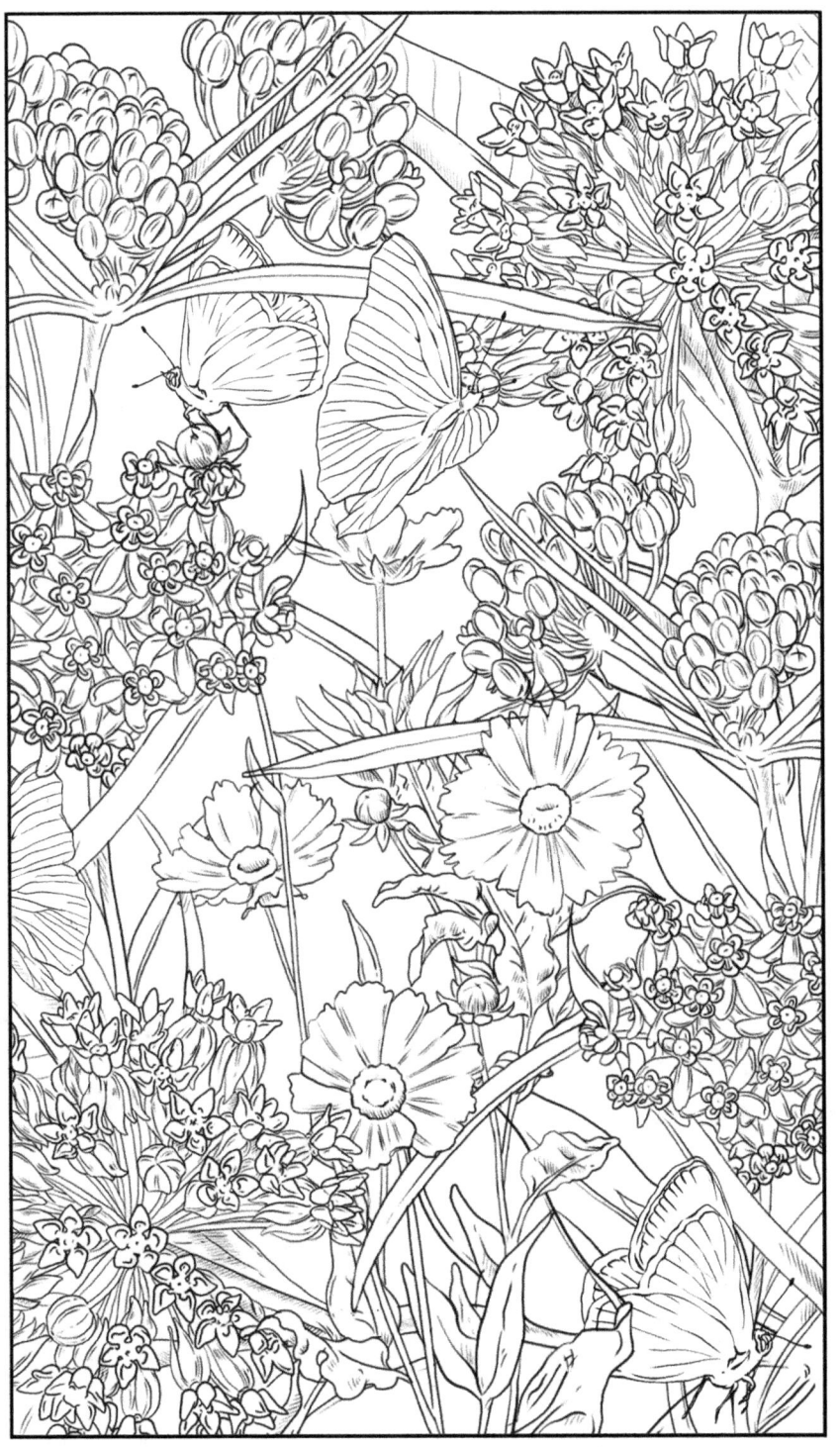

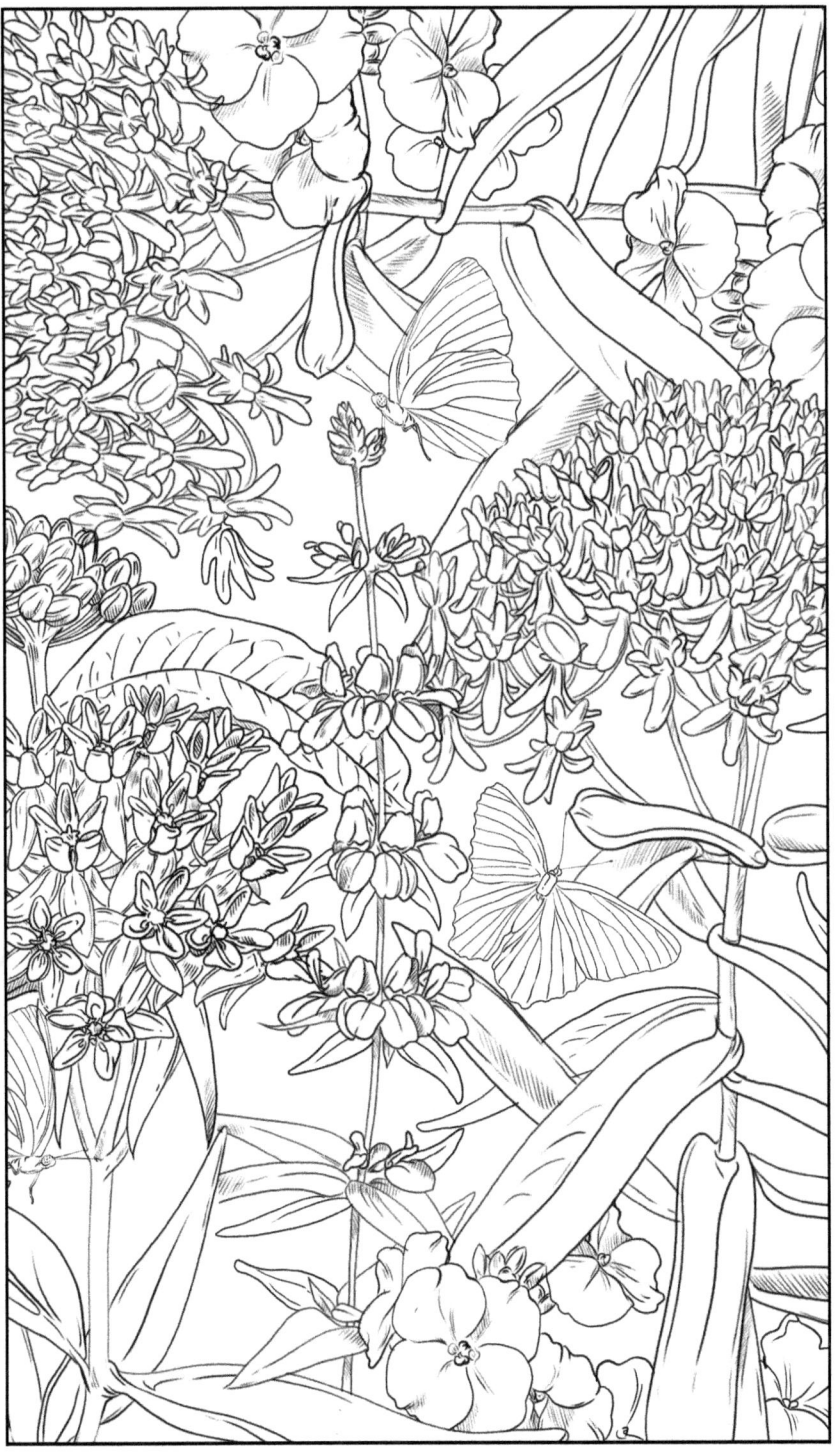

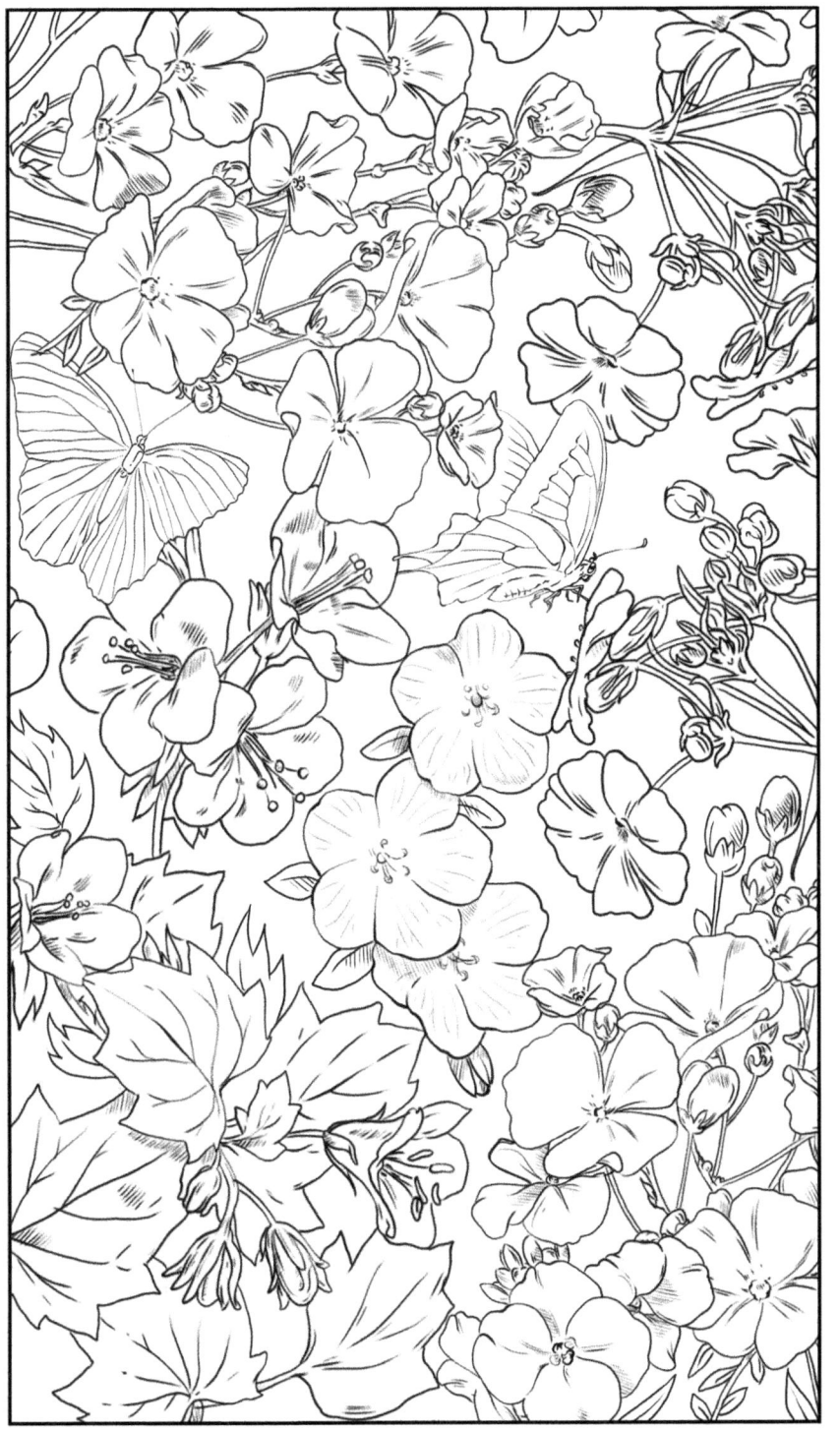

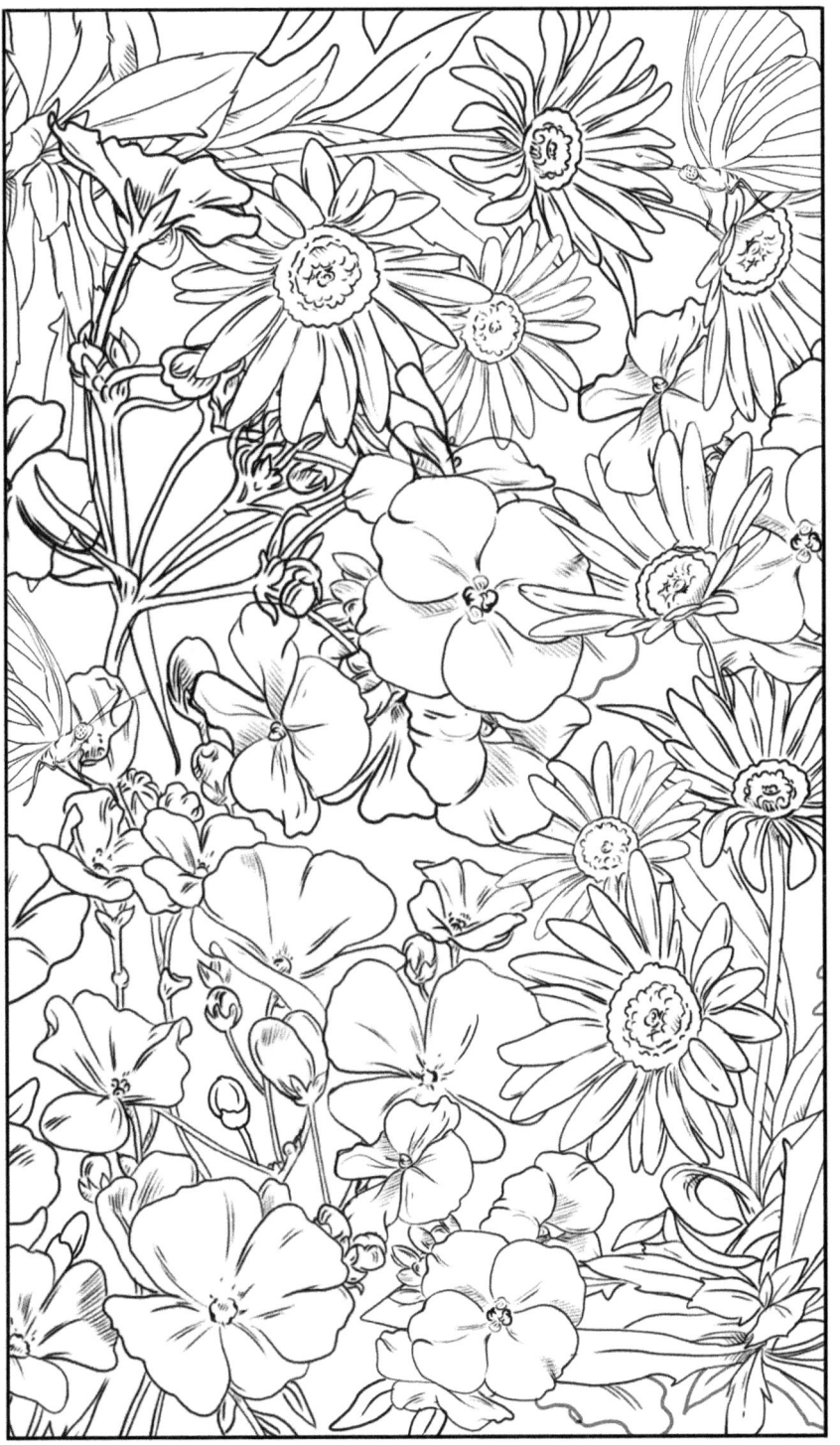

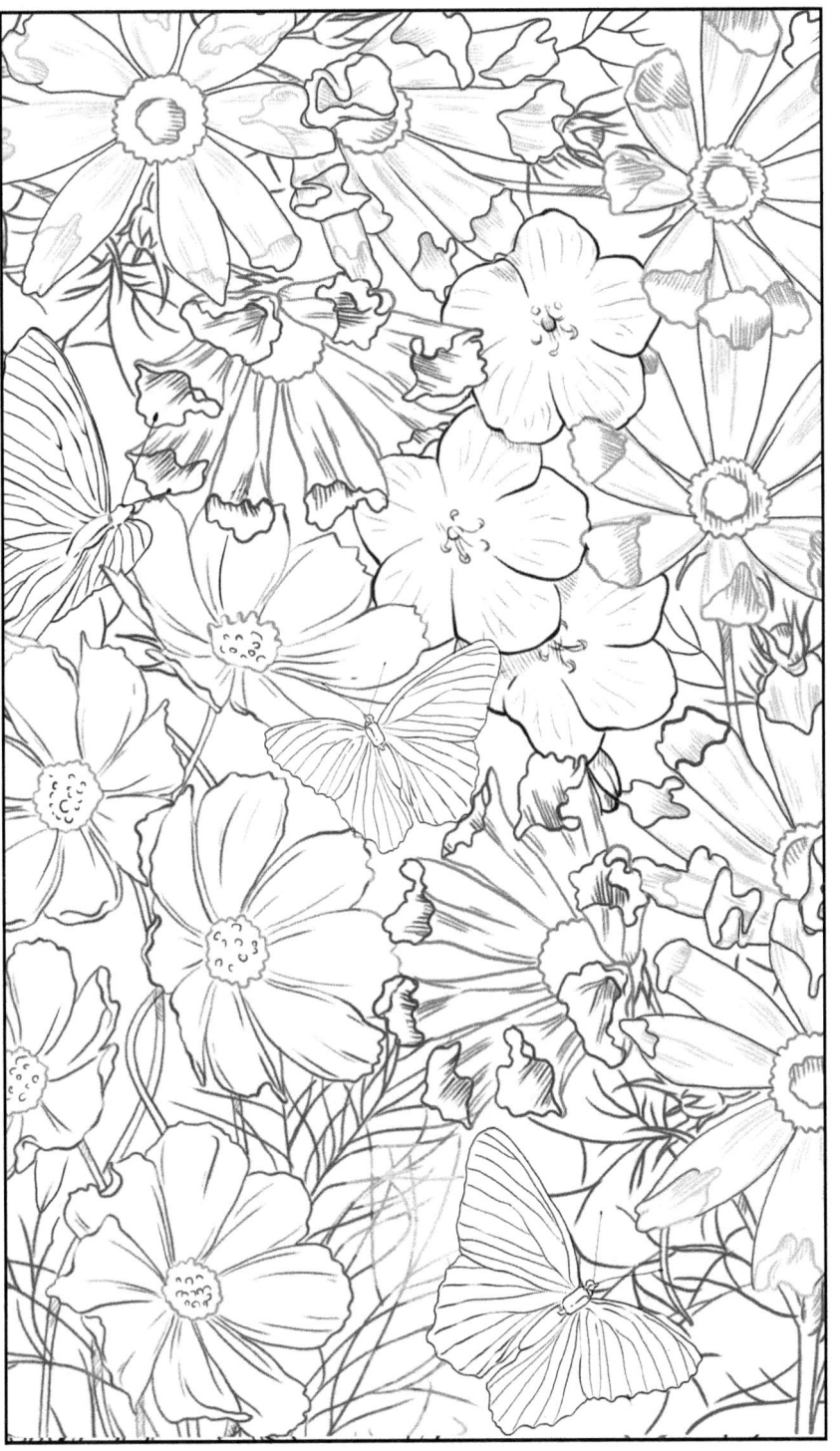

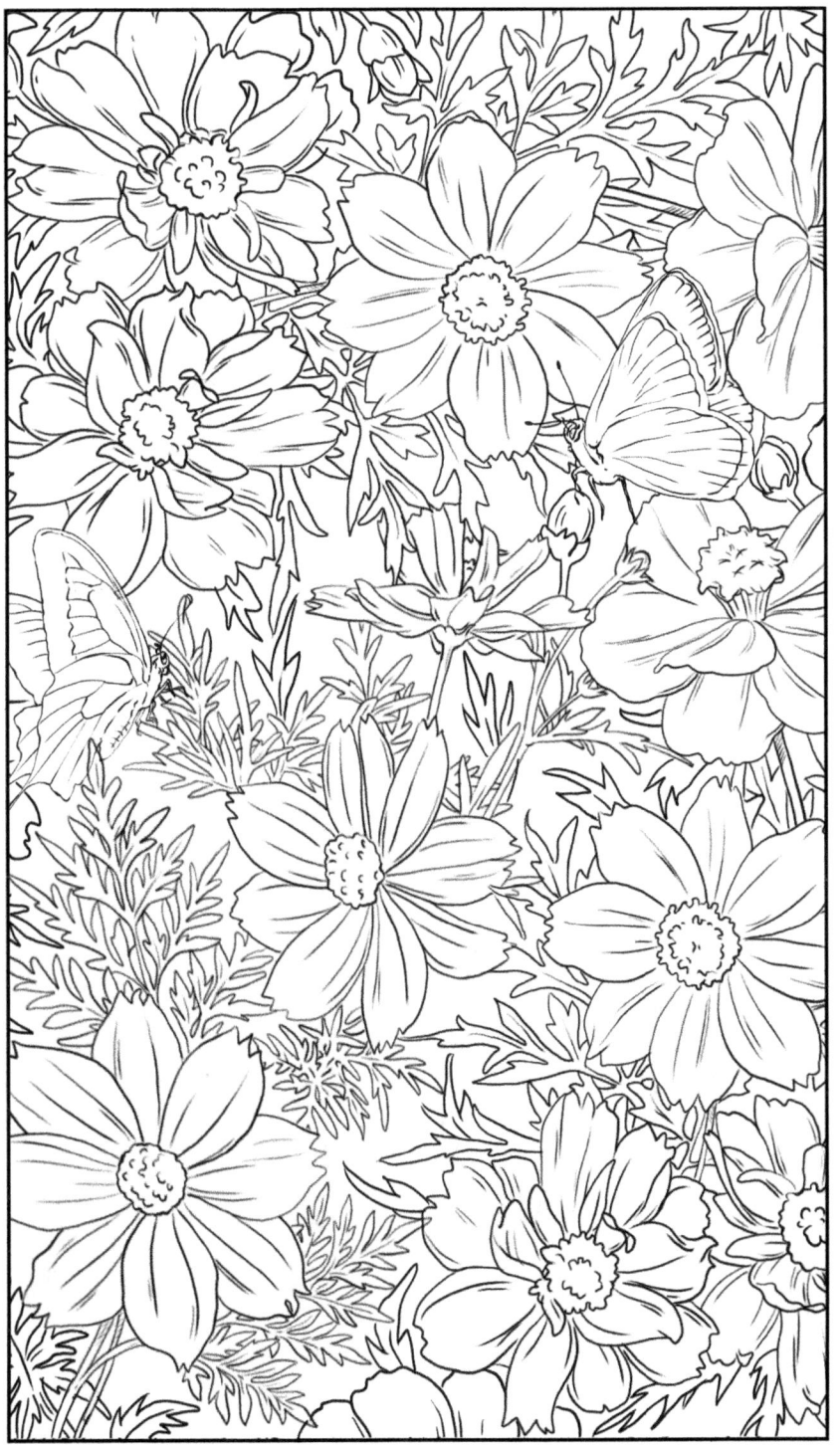

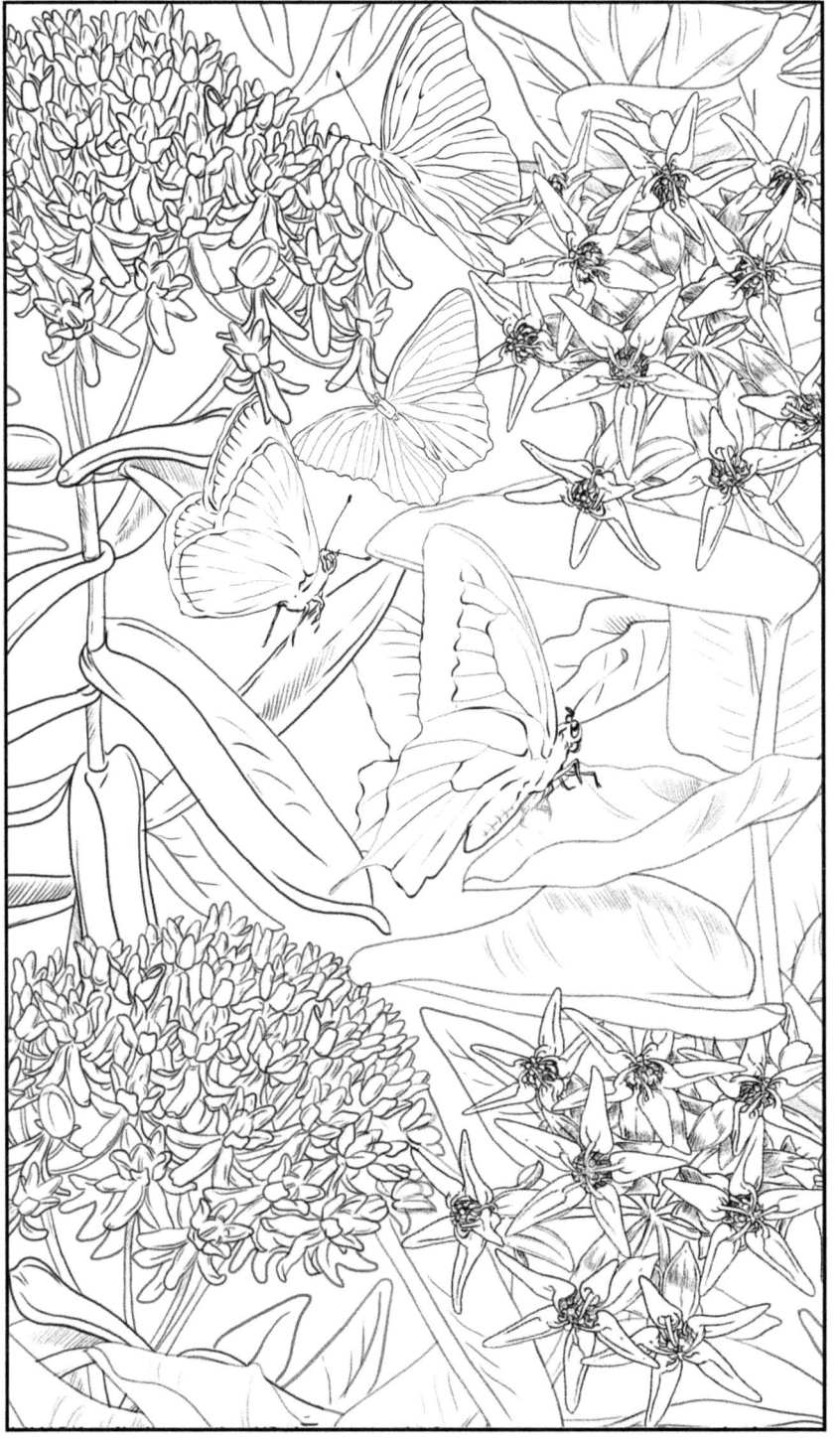

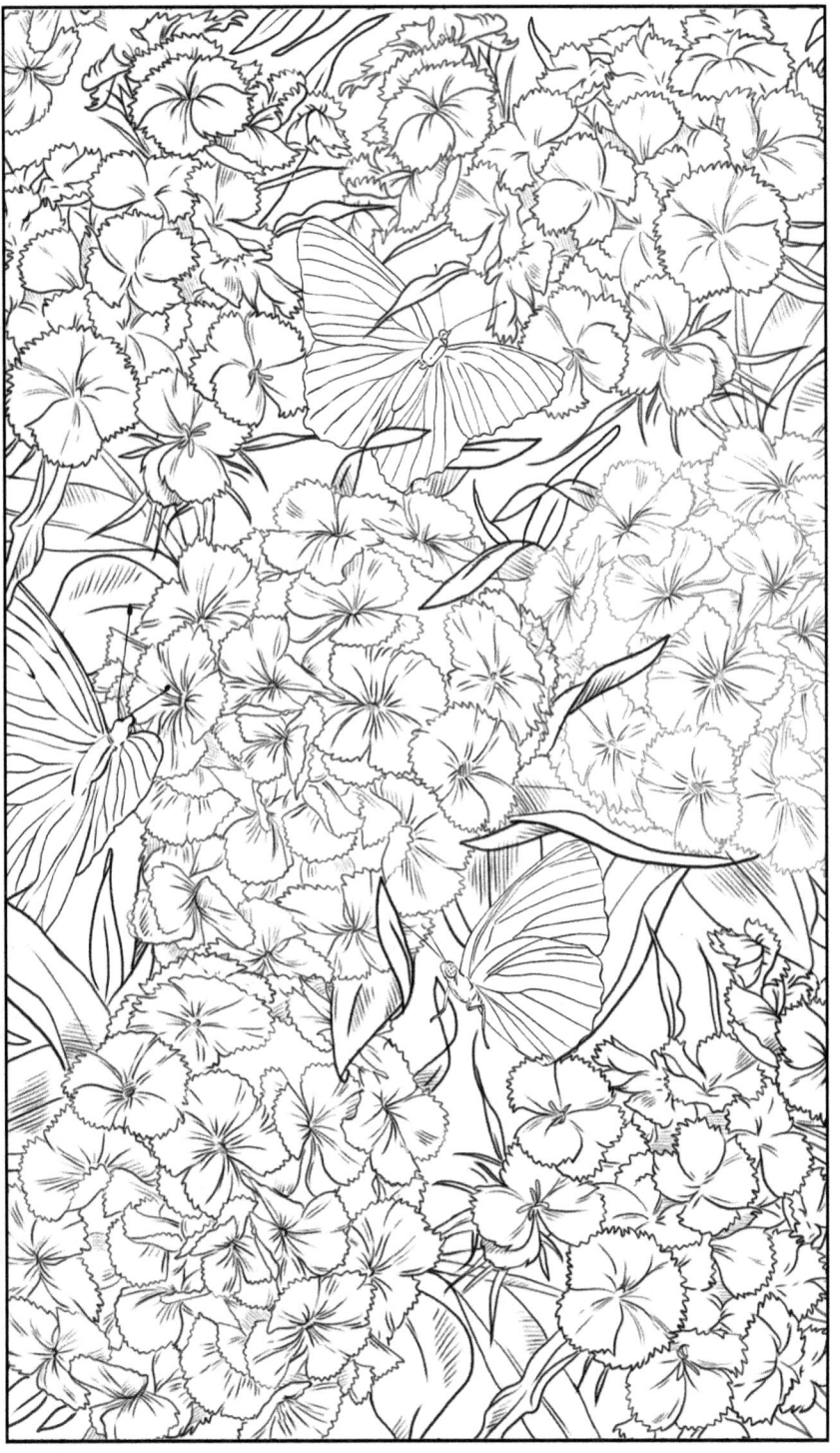

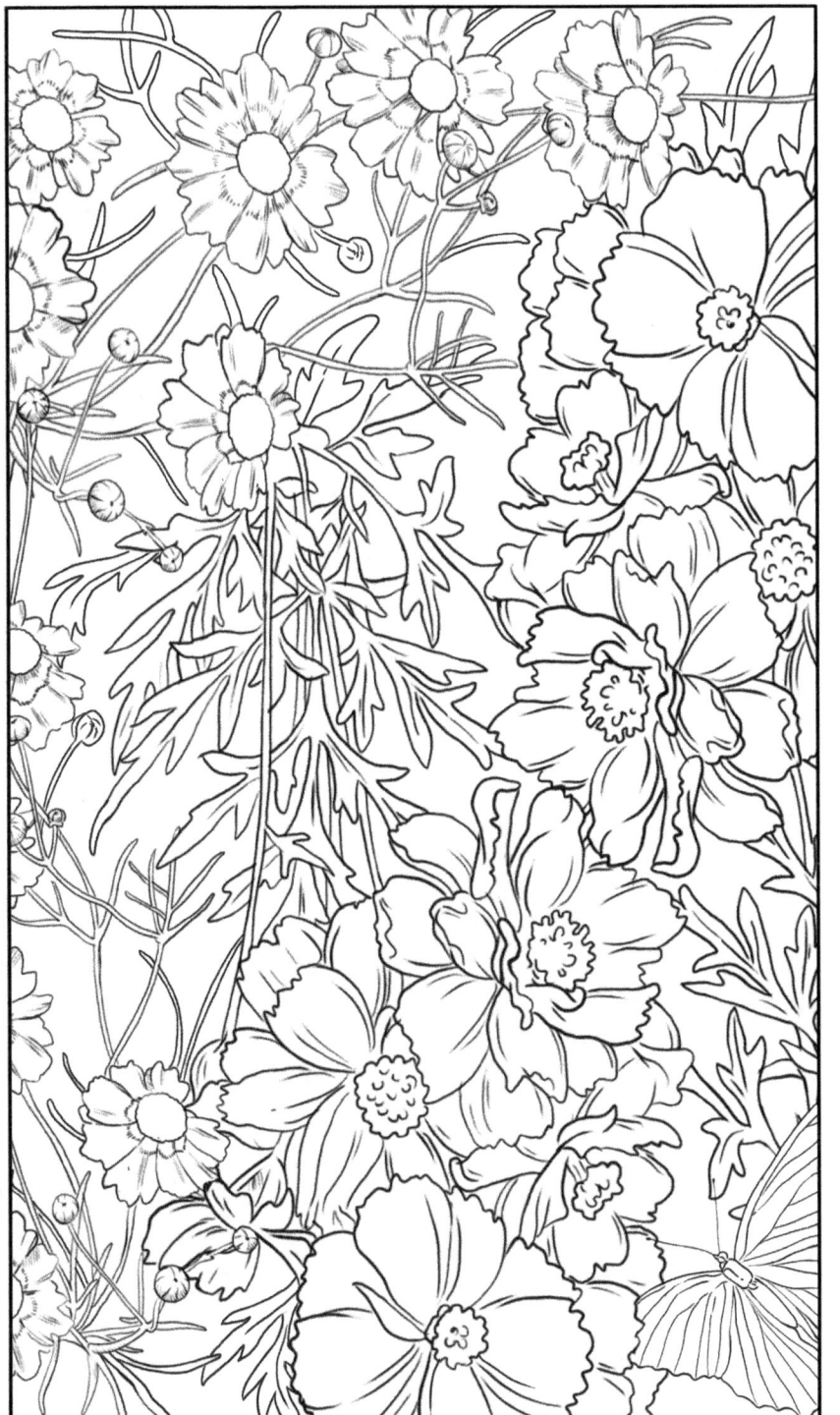

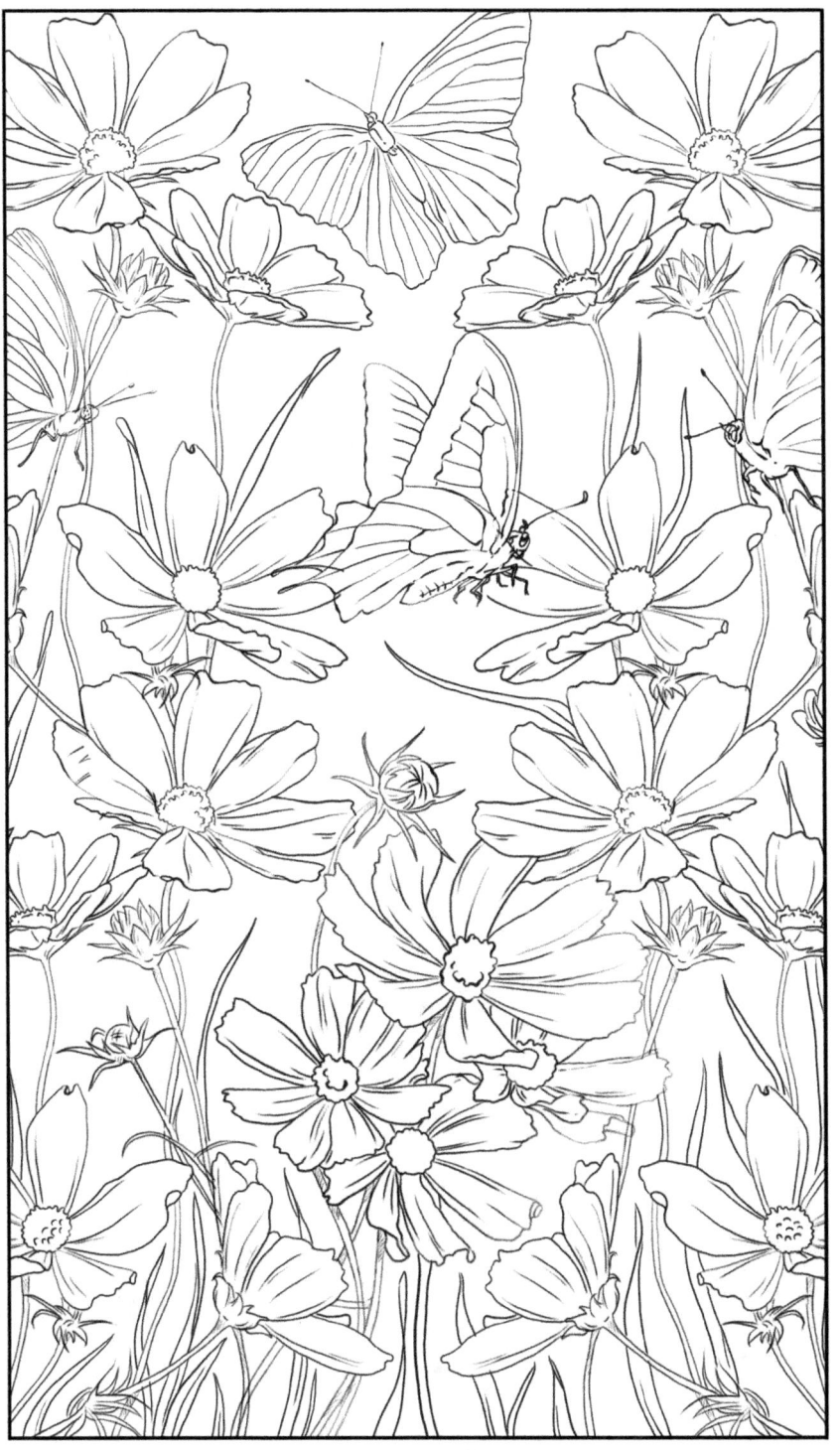

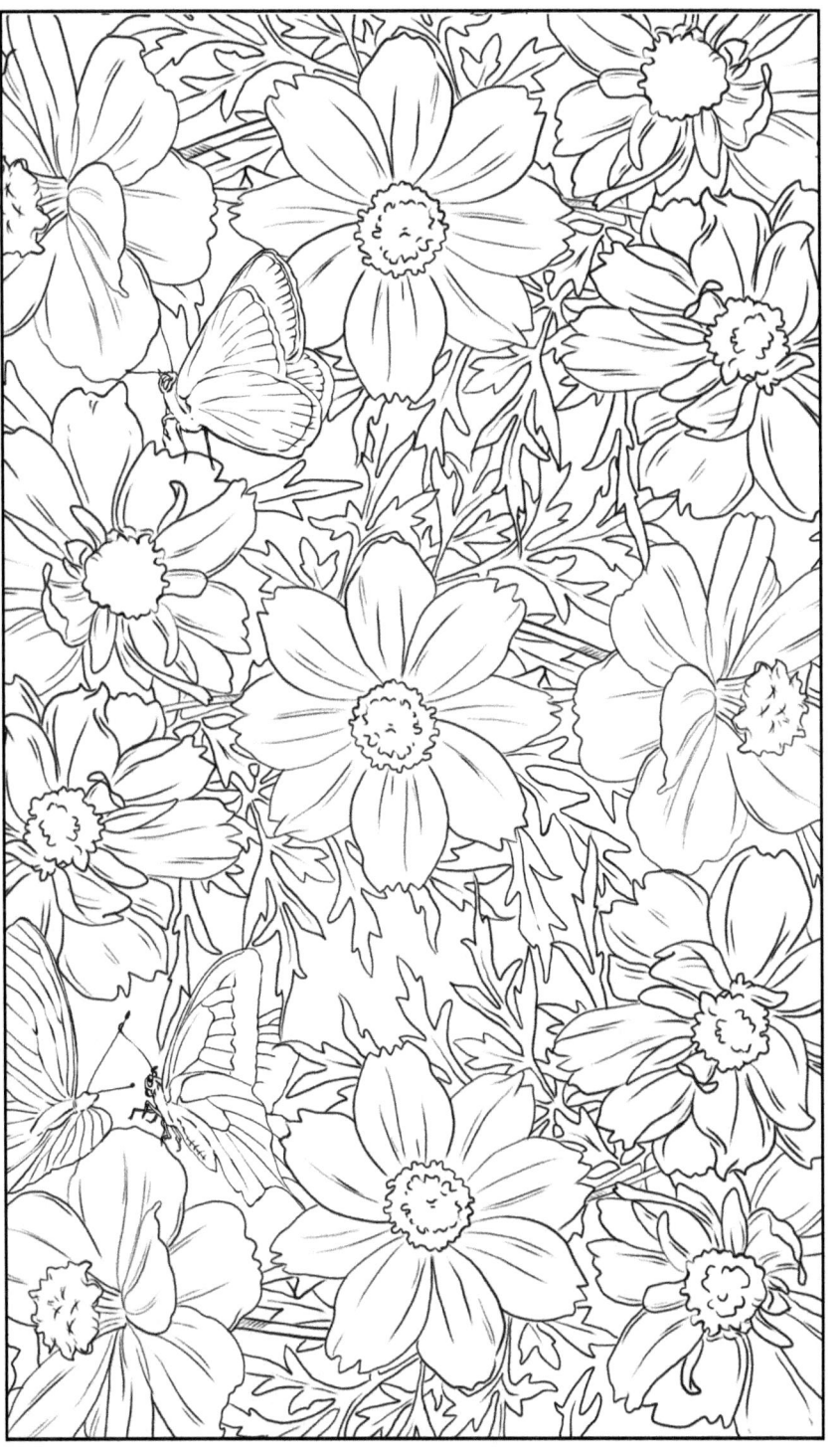

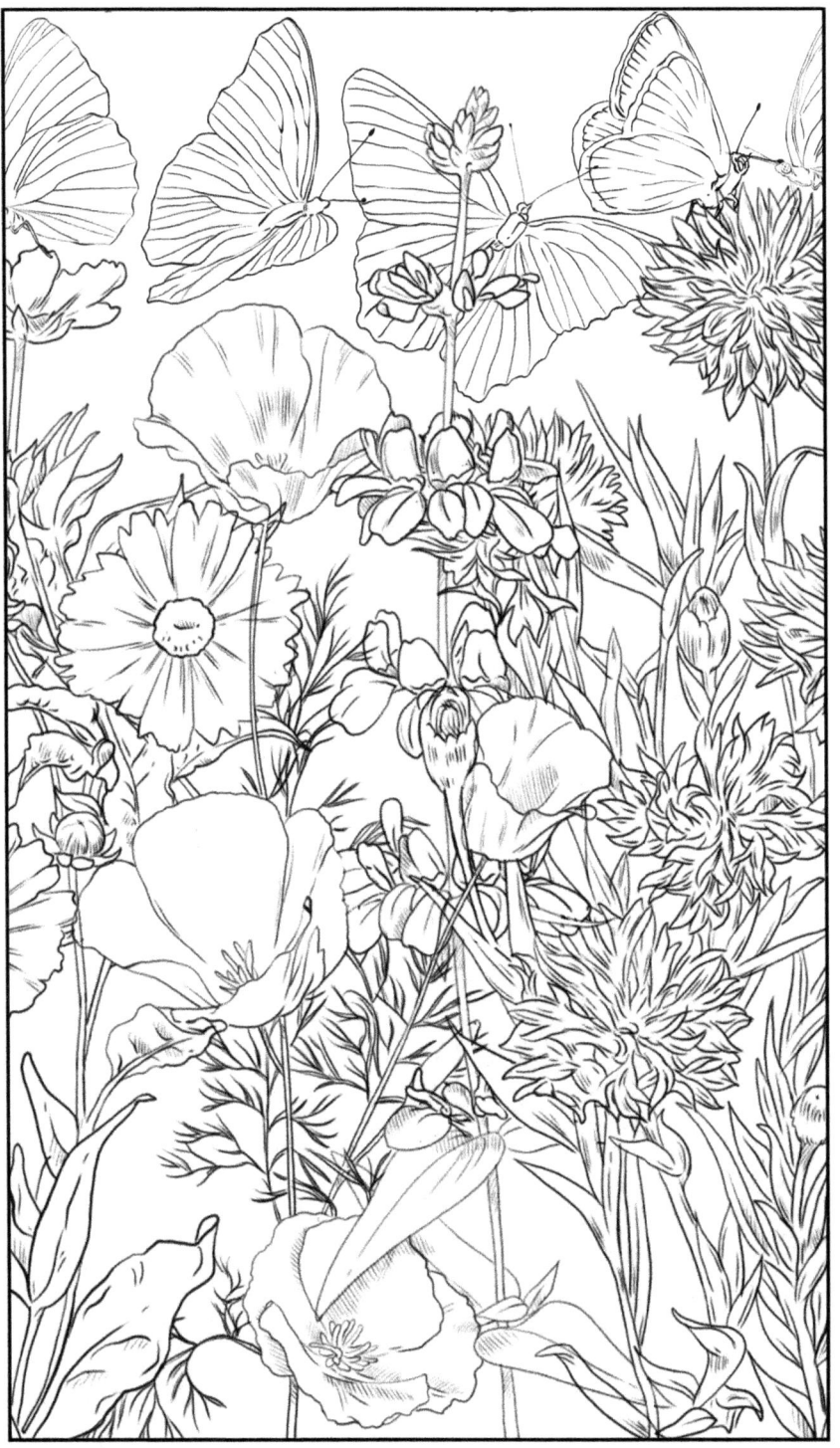

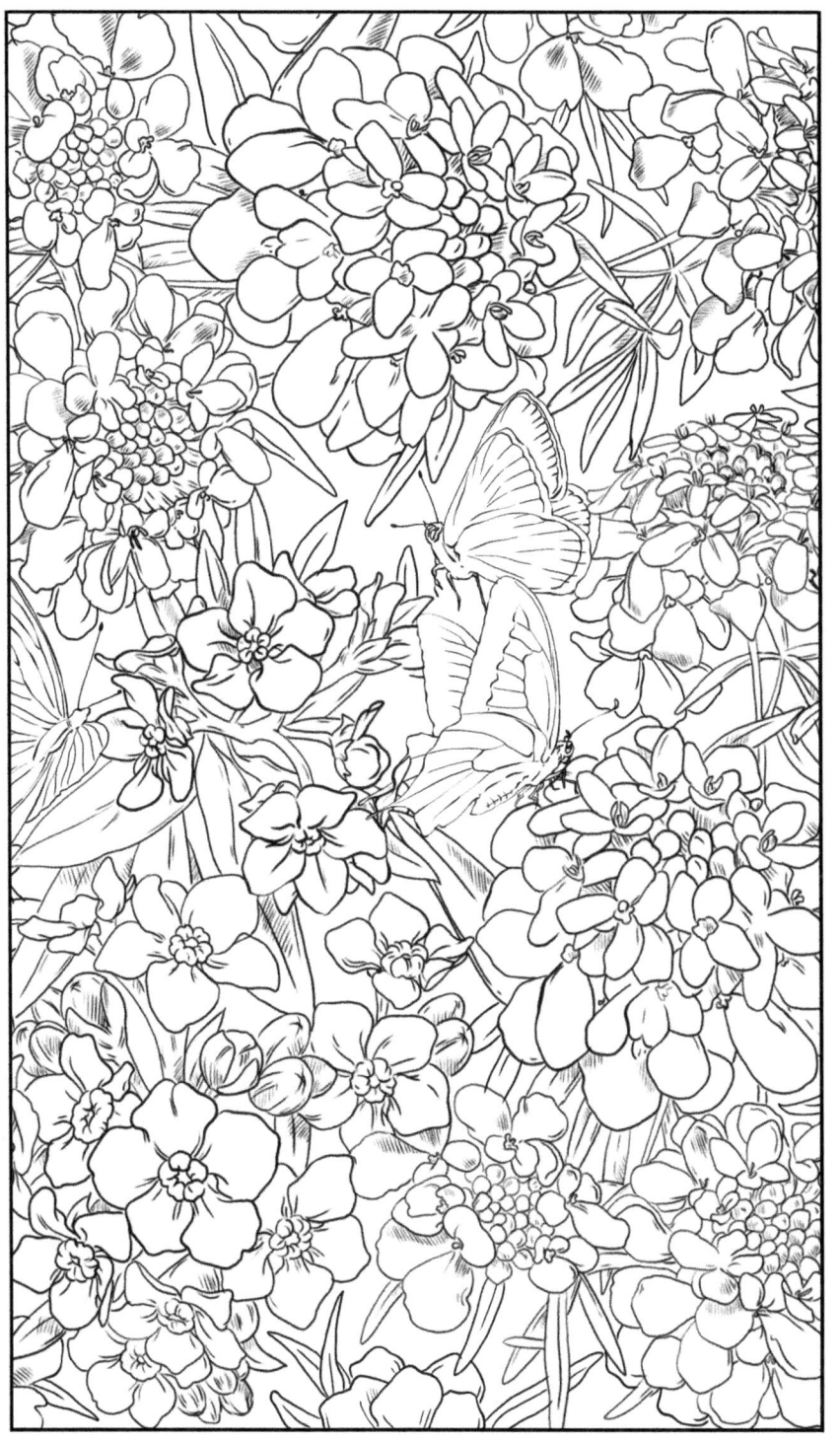

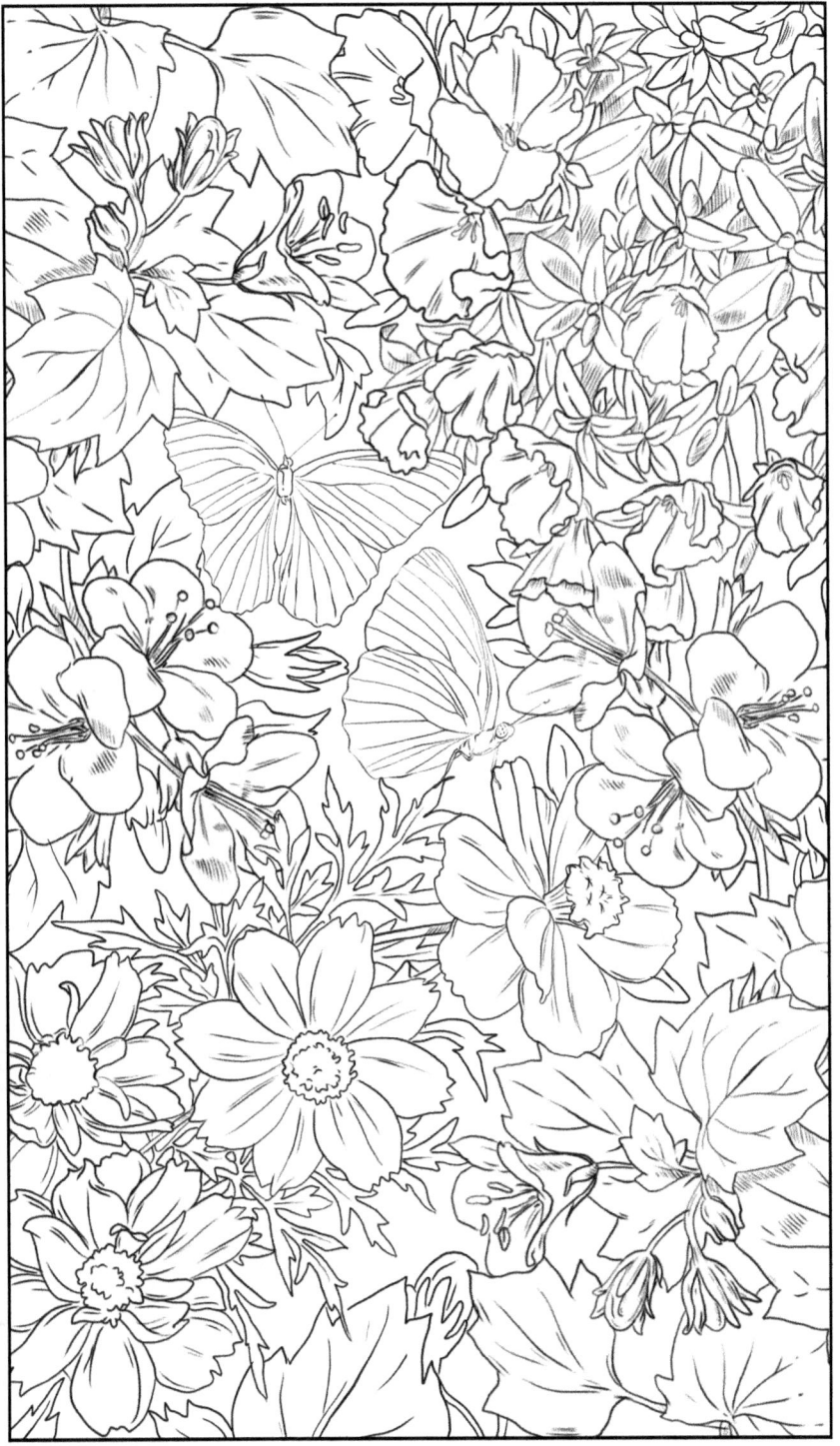

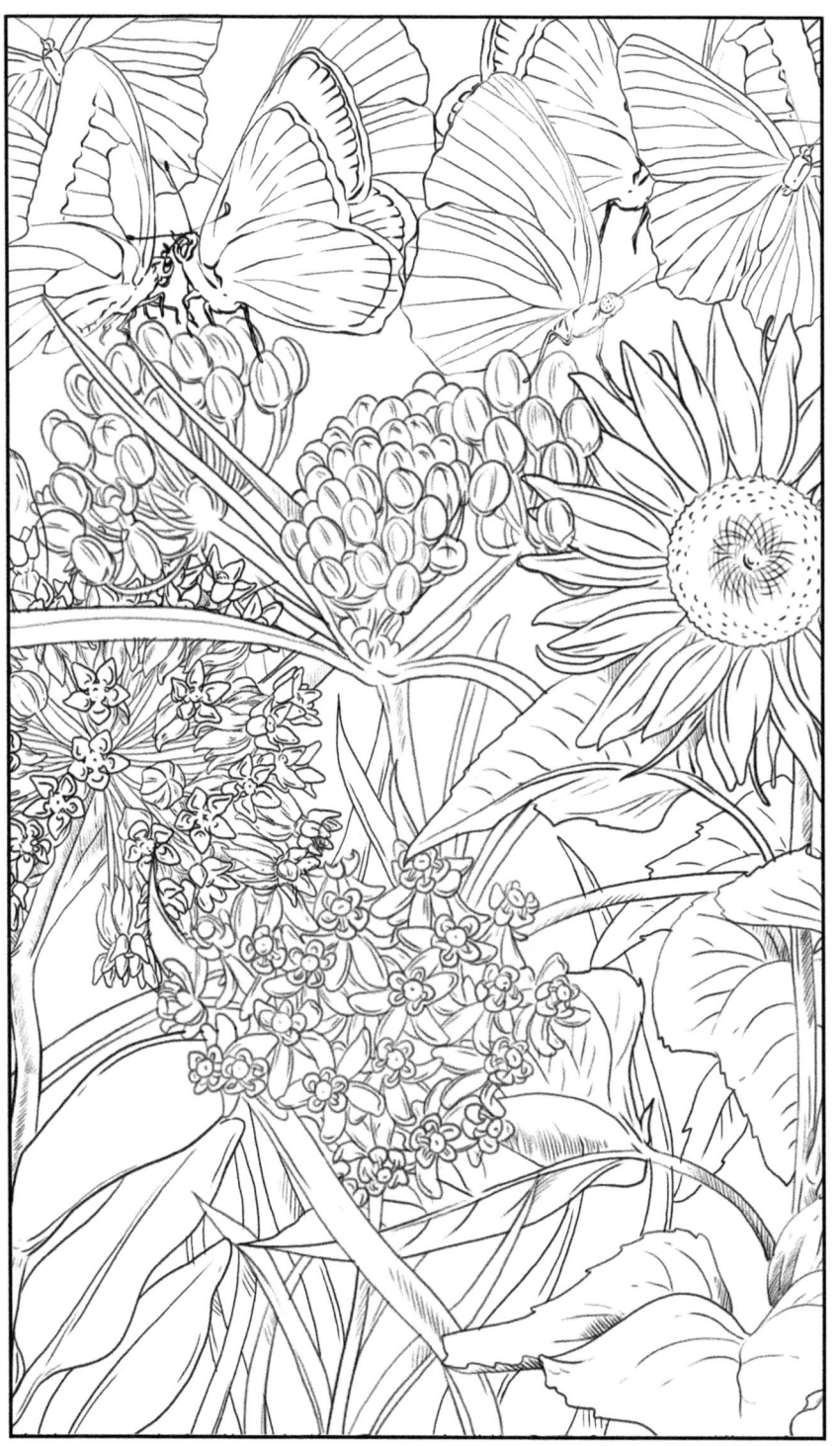

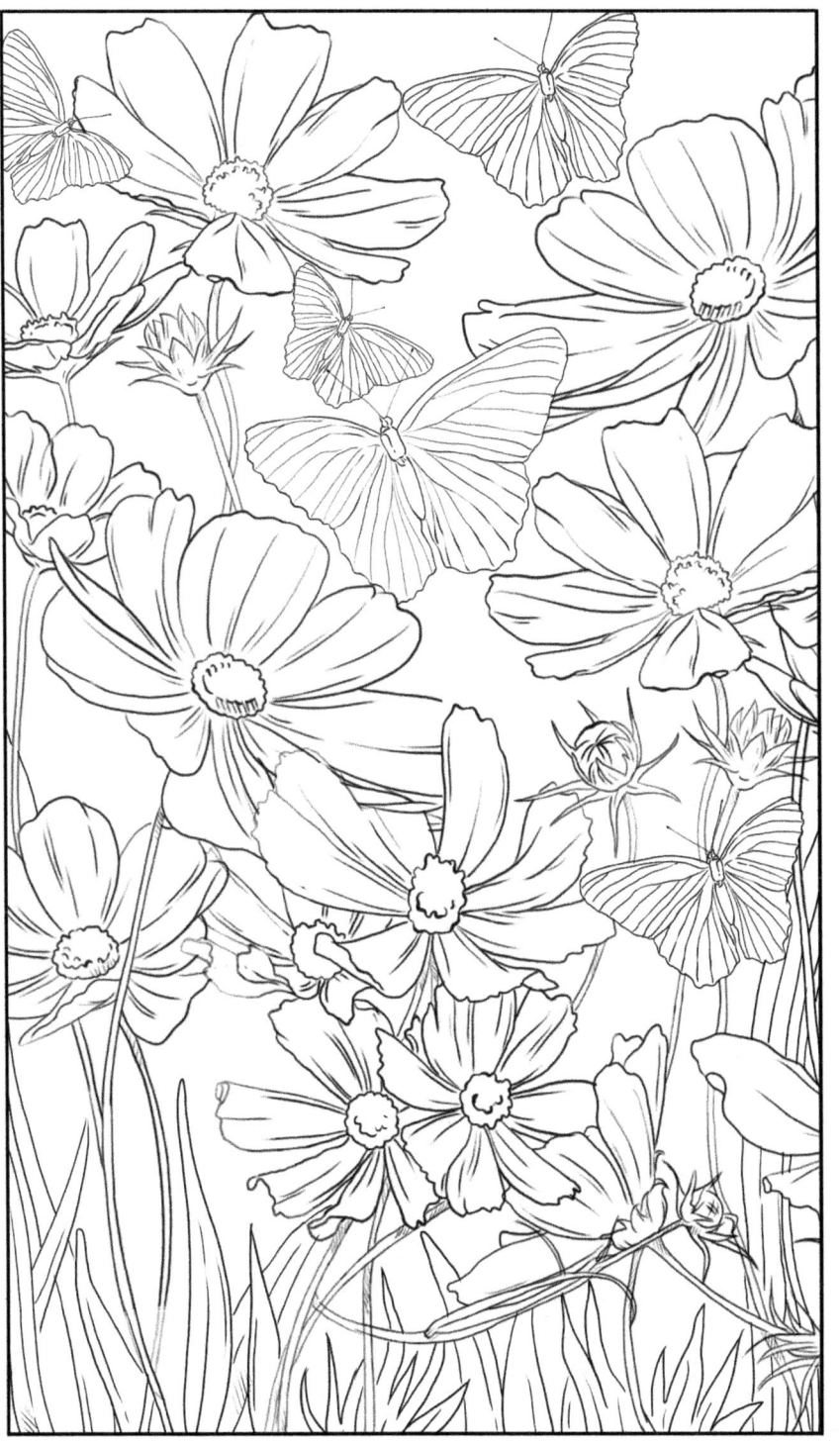

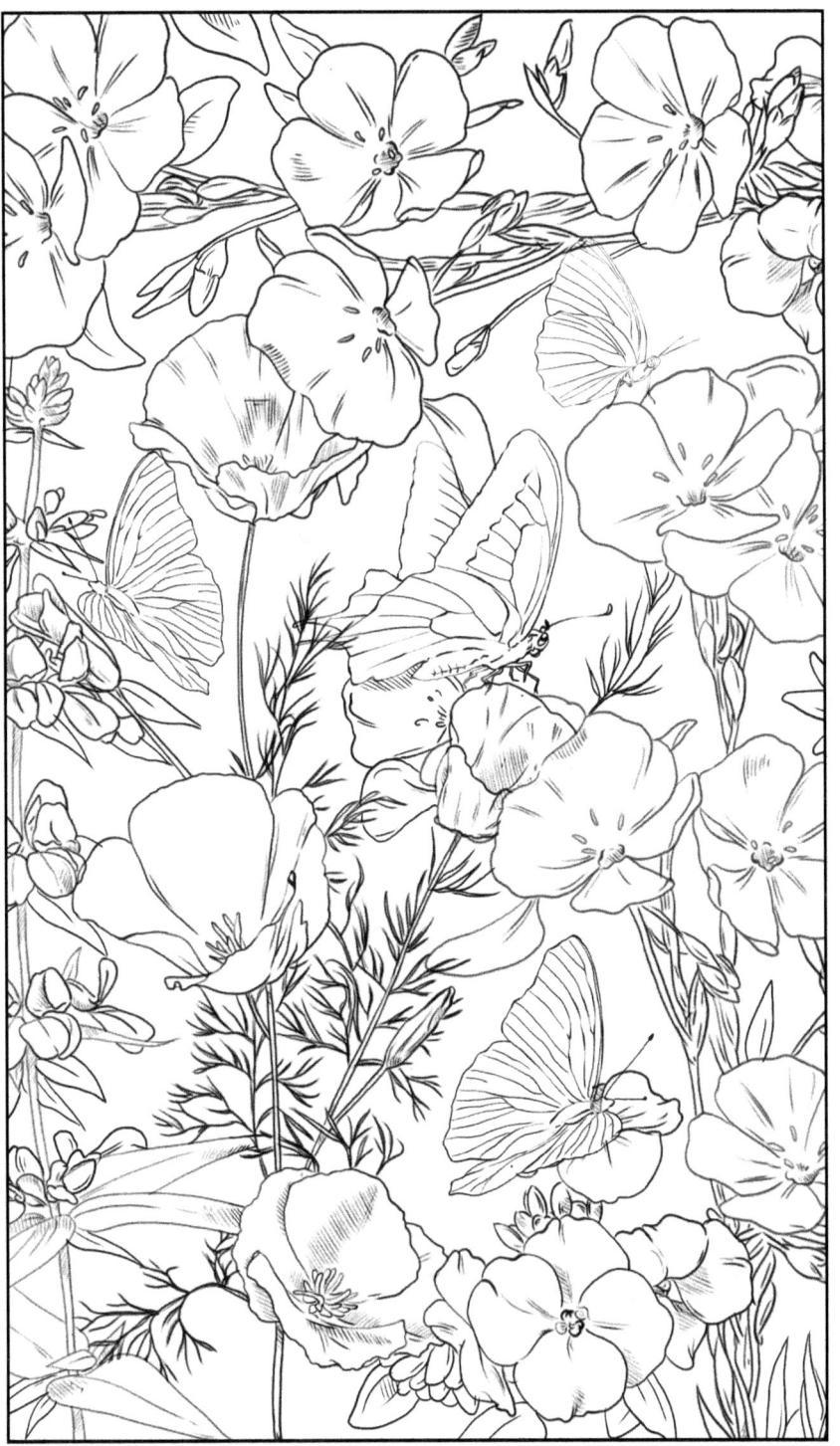

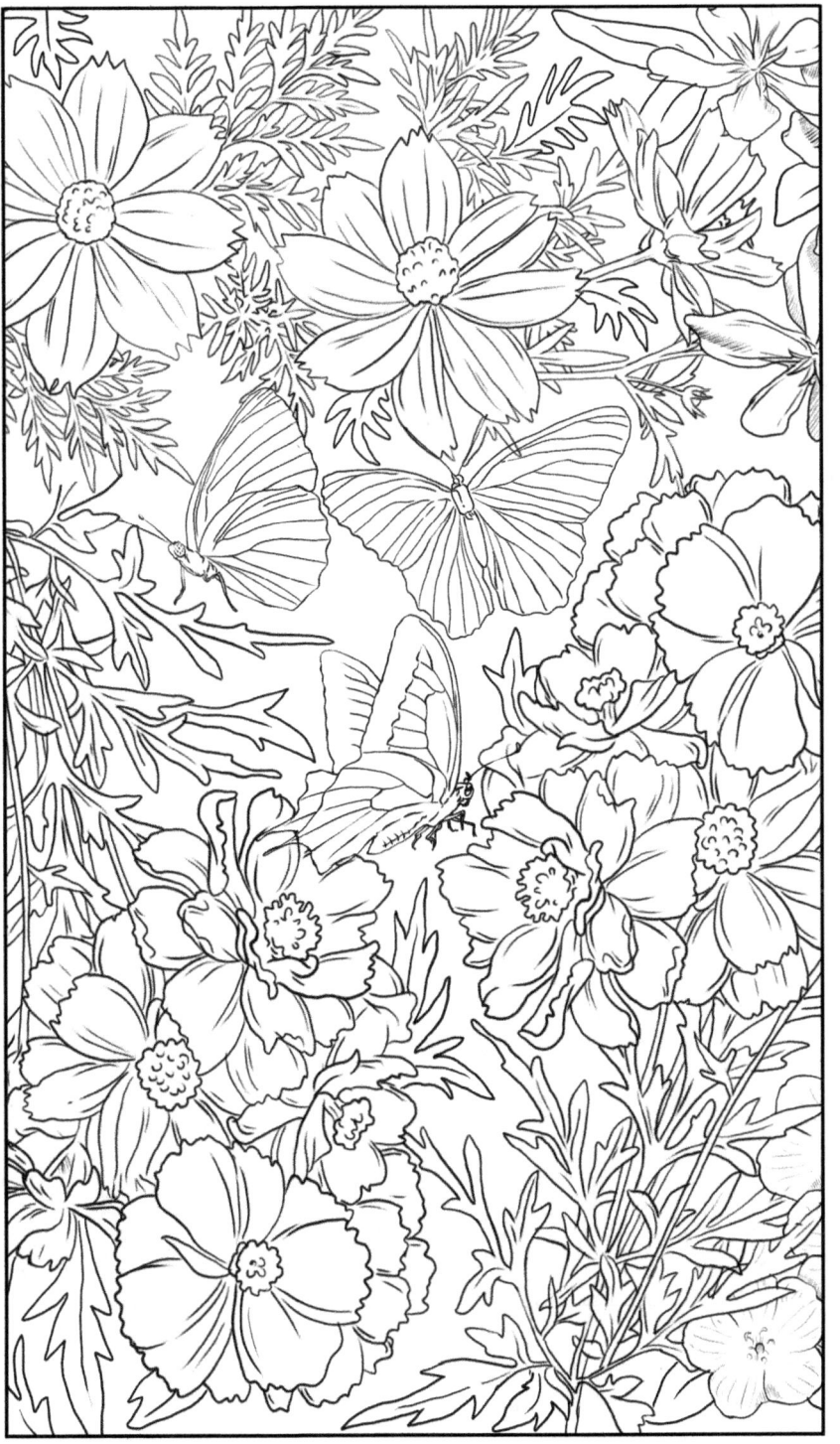

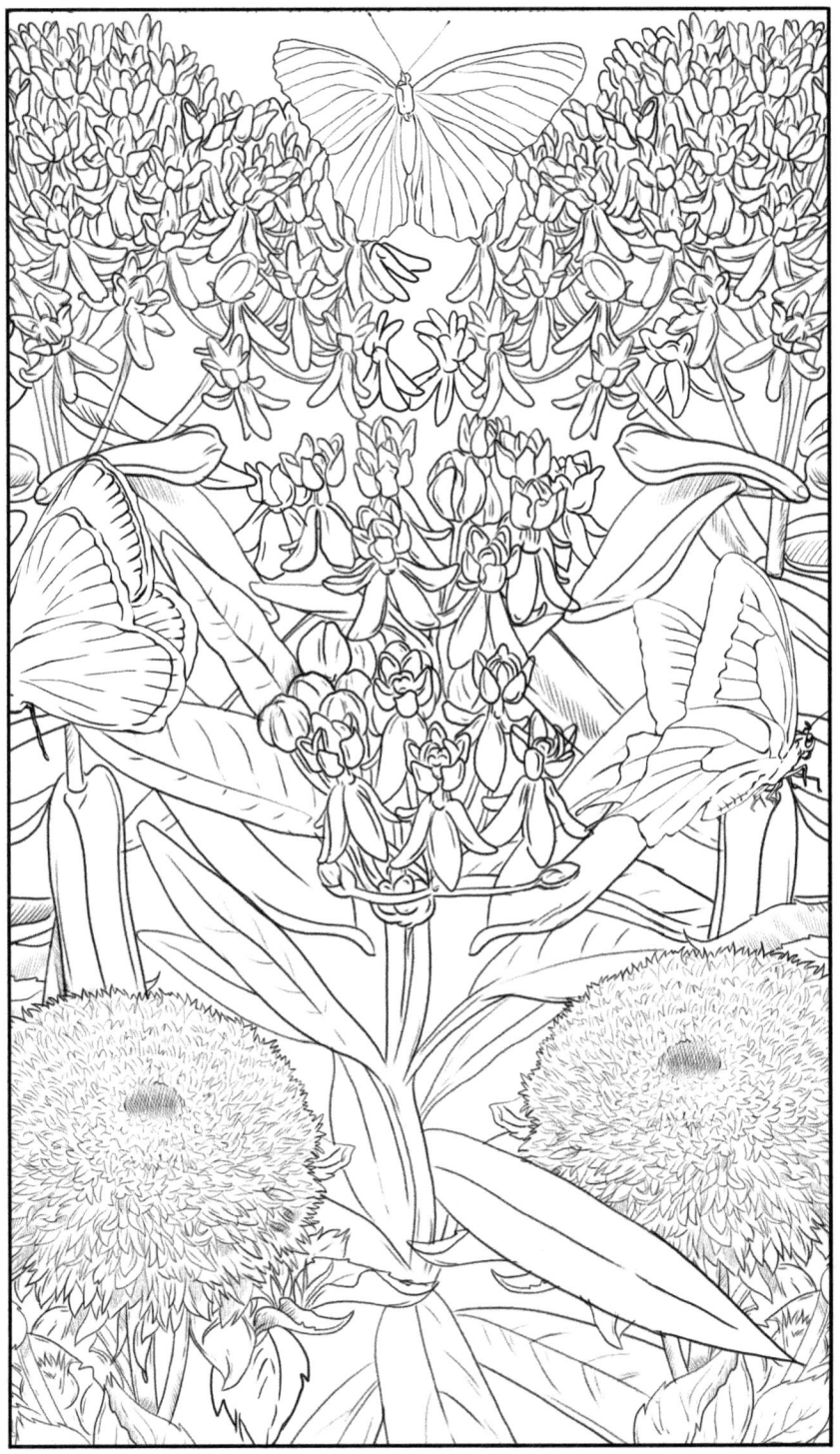

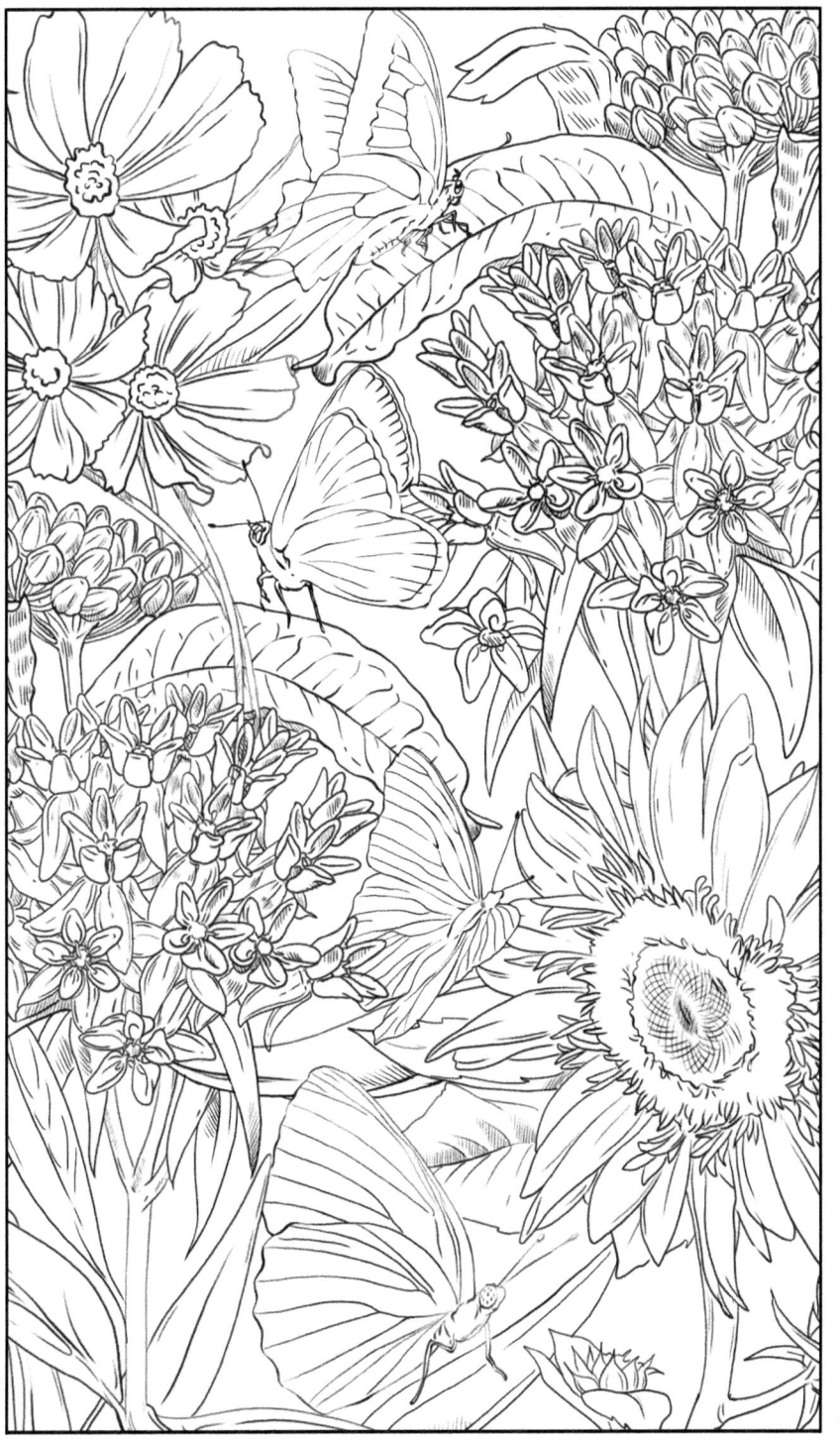

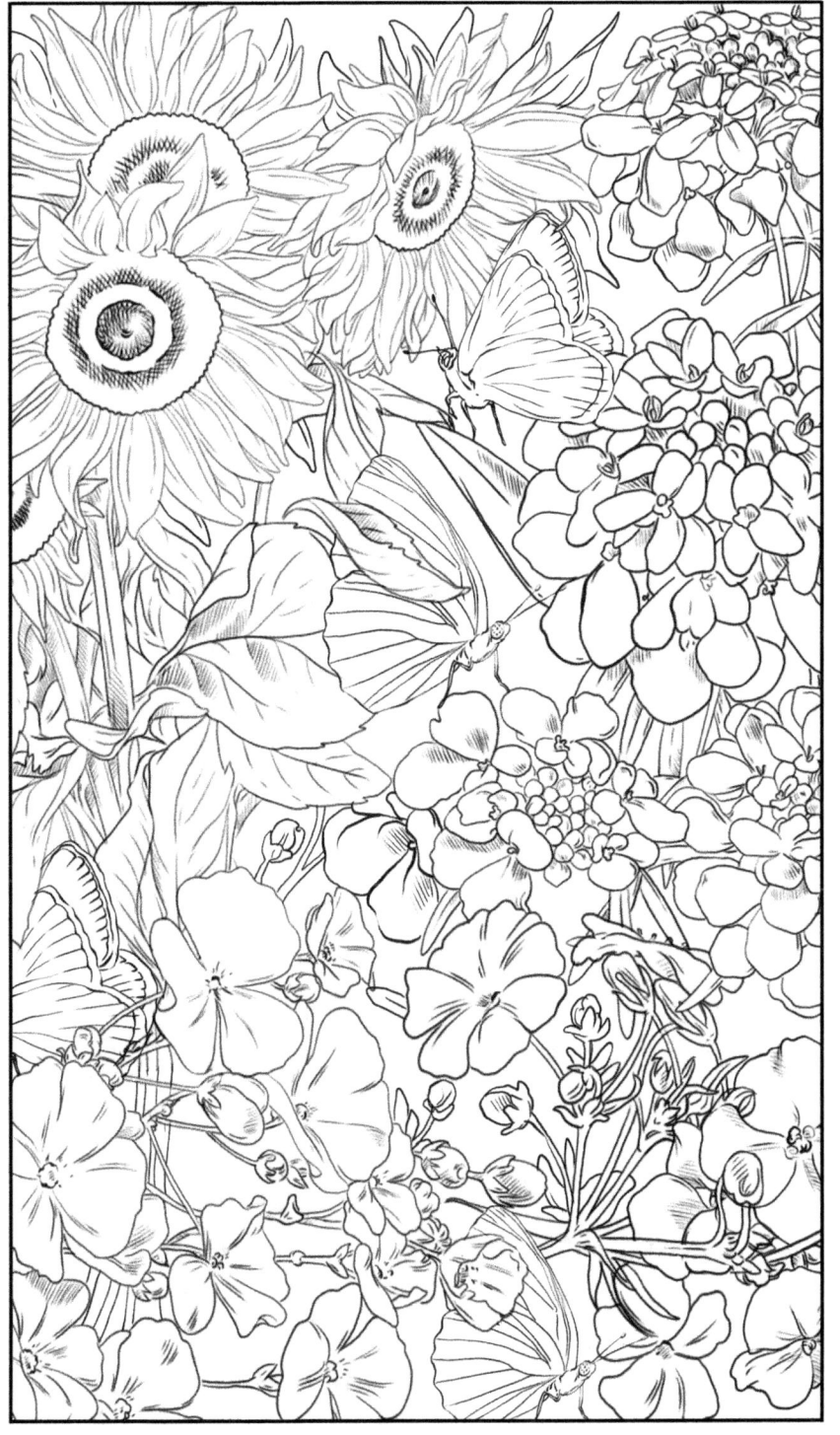

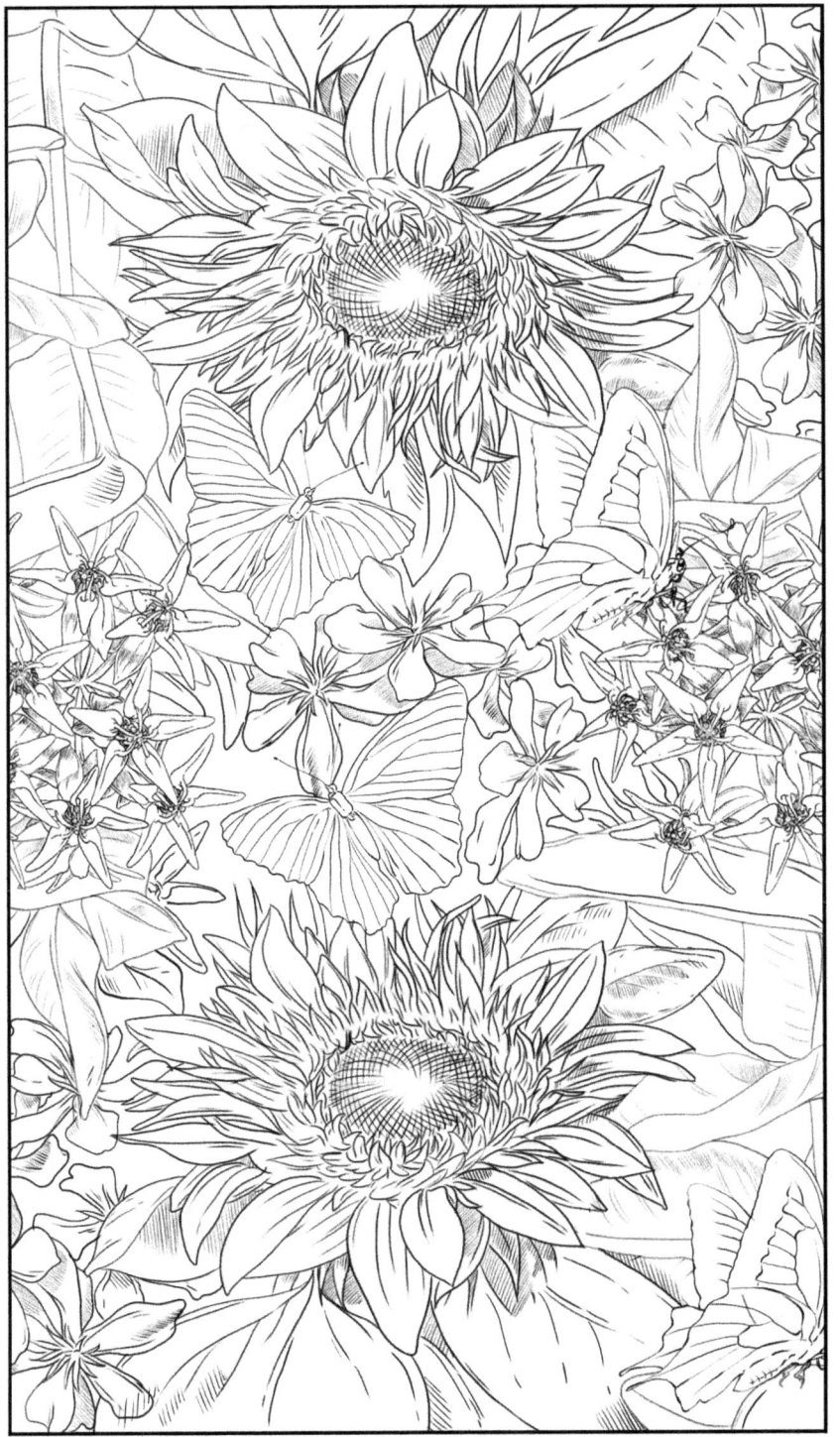

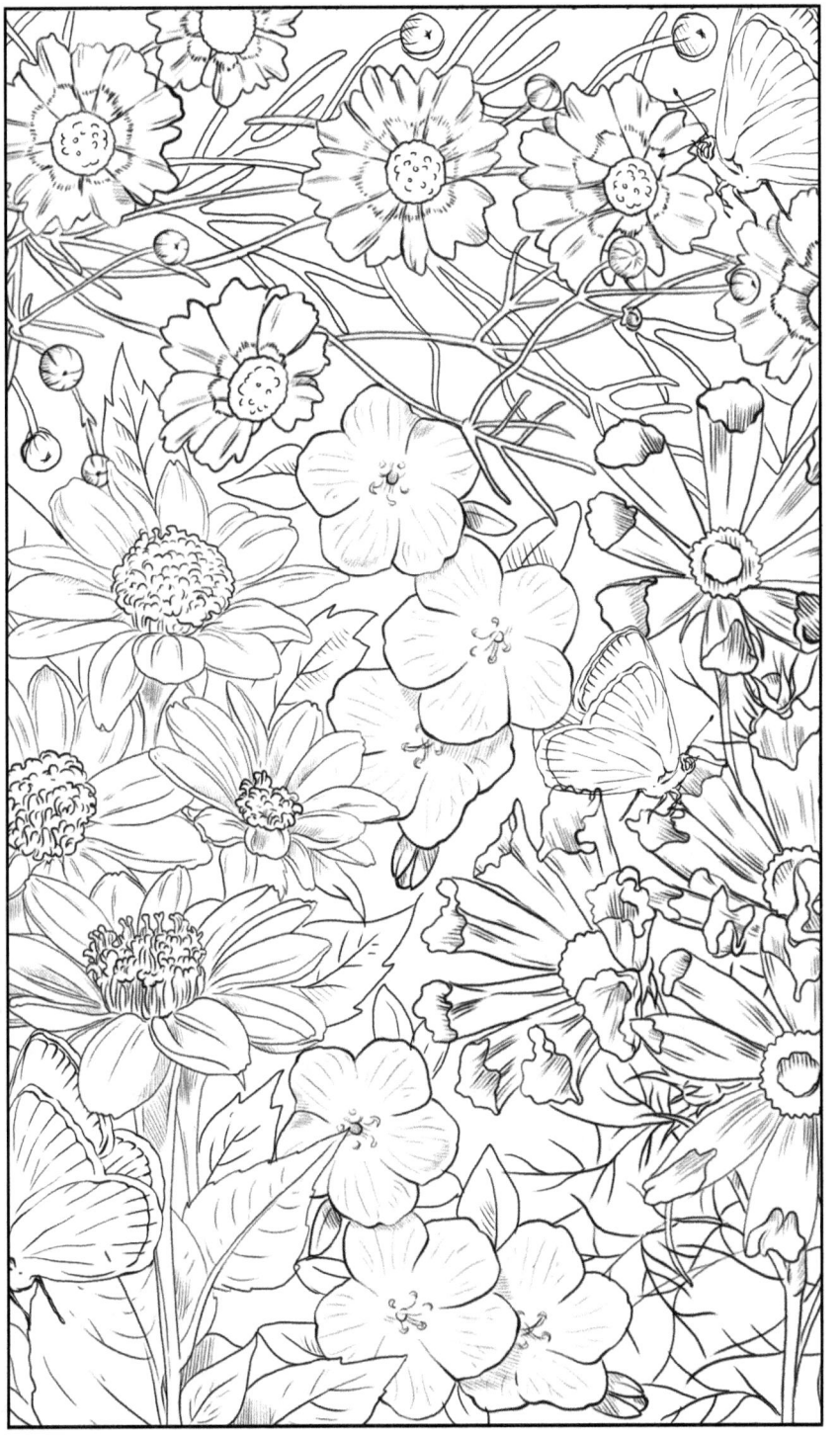

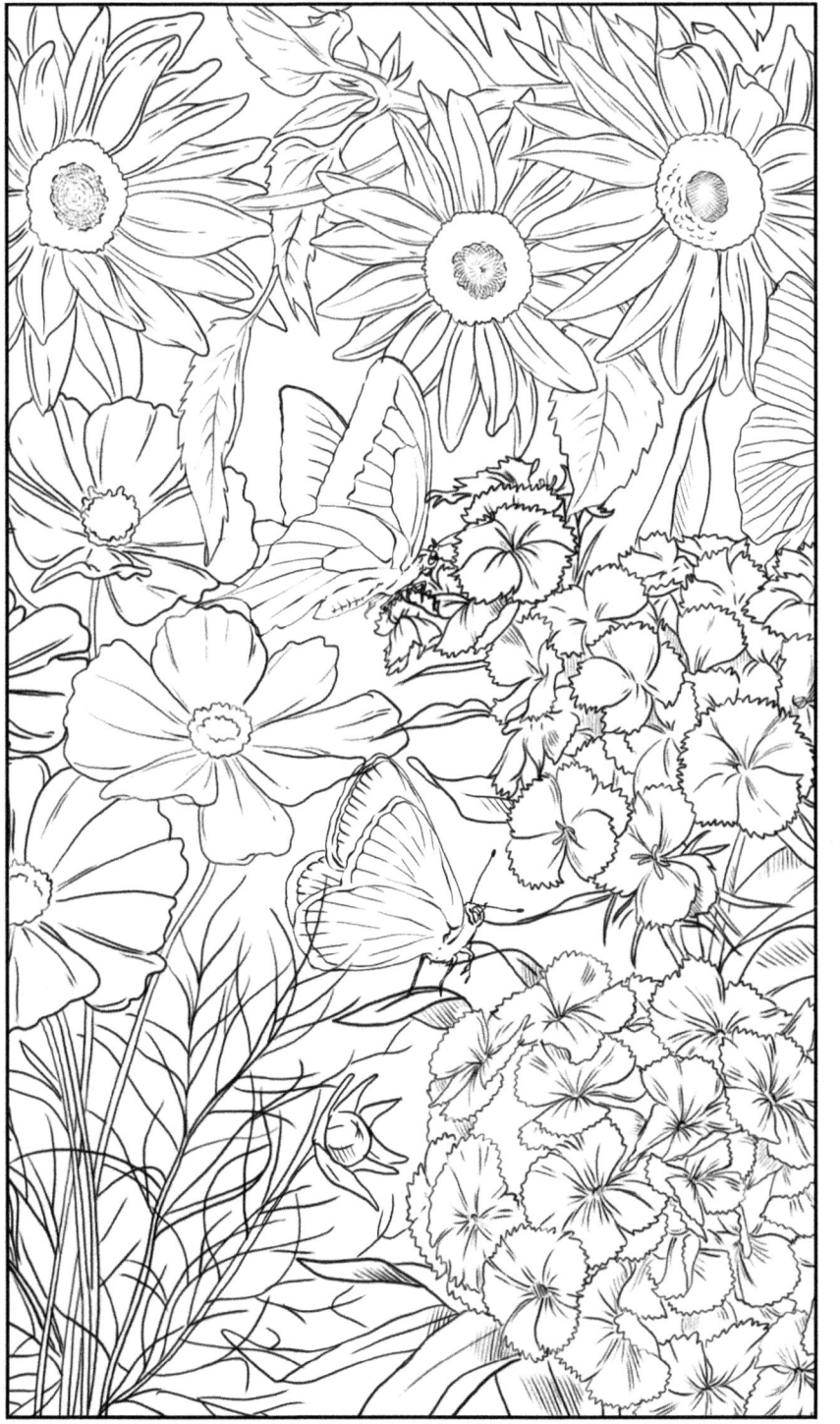